The Daily Telegraph

Seeds
of
Wisdom

The Daily Telegraph

Seeds of Wisdom

Edited by Val Bourne

To Jolyon – for your help and support

First published in Great Britain in 2003
by Cassell Illustrated,
a division of Octopus Publishing Group Limited
2-4 Heron Quays, London E14 4JP

This paperback edition published in 2004 by Cassell Illustrated
Text copyright © Val Bourne 2003
Design and layout copyright © Octopus Publishing Group
Limited 2004

Illustrations by Allan Drummond

A CIP catalogue record for this book is available
from the British Library.

ISBN 1 84403 264 7

Printed in Spain

Foreword

Gardening is not solely concerned with aesthetic
expression, but is an organic process that satisfies our
deep-felt love for the land and our nurturing instincts, as
well as our creative desires. Gardens are privileged spaces
catalysing the relationship between the human being and
his or her natural surroundings, and the gardeners in them
not only need to experience and understand the nature of
the place, but also the principal, underlying factors that
make the place, and the plants within them flourish.
The gardener not only has to play the role of artist and
sculptor, composing the picture but also that of the
nurturing parent. In order to be successful our gardeners
need to possess a vast store of information. They need to
be in touch with the climate, the soil, the plants and the
interlocking ecology of the site, as well as being aware of
its sense of design and history. They need to develop the
capacity and knowledge to understand and interpret all
these aspects. Plants, above all, need special care and
attention, and many of our most successful gardeners

have a 'sixth sense' or are 'green-fingered'. This special skill mustn't be taken for granted. It needs an expert eye and a personal connection with plants that comes into fruition with experience through years of hard work and trial and error. This is a world the highly professional gardener shares with the enthusiastic amateur, where the knowledge gained over the years is exchanged and passed on. Sometimes this knowledge is reorganised, or perhaps reinterpreted, or simply added to with fresh ideas. This exchange of information is of utmost importance, and for each and every gardener gives them the necessary platform to work off.

Val Bourne's collection of gardening tips from some of Britain's most expert and colourful gardeners gives us a fascinating insight into their working lives. Their voices are rich, varied and cover all aspects of gardening. The contributors include prestigious garden designers, Curators and Superintendents of well-known institutions, Head Gardeners and Assistants of large and small private and public gardens, as well as the expert amateur. The places and the people may vary but the overall goal is always the same: to create a place of individual beauty that gives pleasure not only to the people in them but also to the visitor.

The aptly named *Seeds of Wisdom* is a unique collection of expertise. From snippets of advice on design, plant association, pests and diseases, working in bad weather, pruning, staking and feeding, seed sowing and propagating, to even choosing the right dog, a whole range of subjects are dipped into. You may simply be advised 'never go into the garden without your secateurs' (Lord Carrington), or to 'be more adventurous' (Nick Biddle – English Heritage), or told how to sow Monkey Puzzle seeds without them rotting (Paul Champion – Bicton College), the advice is always personal and practical. Some may prefer to use coir in their compost, others vermiculite or an old fashioned 'John Innes' mix. Some companion plant, or stroke their seedlings to make them stronger, others plant in naturalistic drifts and not in clumps. Clive Cox of the National Trust's Kingston Lacey, plants wood anemones amongst deciduous ferns. The anemones flower before the ferns are up, and are later covered by the unfurling fern crosiers, the anemones remaining happily dormant under the ferns until the following year.

Each page is filled with fascinating information, introduced, contextualised, and skilfully linked with Val Bourne's words. As a practising gardener I found this book a joy to read, I hope you will too.

Fergus Garrett

Every gardener is keen to make a start in the garden once the evenings begin to draw out. By mid-February the sun has moments of real warmth, producing feelings of restlessness among gardeners who know that they are coming up to the busiest time of the year. Learning to recognize the moment when spring actually arrives is one of the greatest gardening skills and it's so easy to get it wrong. Sow too early and your seeds will either rot in the soil or, if they do germinate, the new shoots will be picked off by voracious pigeons or rapacious gastropods looking for an early meal.

This first piece of advice is also the shortest in the book. Surprisingly, it's from an ex-politician – a breed not usually known for verbal reticence. It is excellent advice however.

Never go into your garden without your secateurs!

Lord Carrington of The Manor House, Bledlow, Princes Risborough, Buckinghamshire

Those secateurs could be needed sooner than you think. I wear mine in a belted holster, which might make me look a bit like someone out of *Annie-get-your-Gun*, but it's the only way I can stop myself from losing these vital (and very expensive) pieces of gardening kit.

Spring is the perfect time to check your young trees as the winter can kill the growing points. Look carefully at the branches and cut away any dead wood, which will be really visible at this time of the year. If your tree has been staked for a couple of seasons, it may well be able to manage without a stake now. Loosen the tie and try to assess whether or not there is a firmly fixed rootball. If there is, remove the stake. If the stake is still needed, reposition the tie allowing enough leeway for the tree to grow. A tree stake does not keep the trunk straight – it is there to stop the roots moving.

Mark Flanagan, Keeper of the Savill Garden and The Valley Gardens, Windsor Great Park, Surrey

Cherry trees need to wait until later in the year, though.

 Cherry trees should only be pruned during June when the sap is flowing freely. This seals the wounds quickly so preventing disease from entering. Prune at other times of the year and you will introduce infections and diseases. Silver-leaf disease, which can enter through cuts and other damage, is one of the most devastating and to be avoided at all costs.

Andrew McCoryn and the team at Coleton Fishacre Garden (T

David Beaumont is busy cutting some lengths of birch to weave together into turban-shaped structures. More decorative than tripods, these are used to support fragrant sweet peas.

Birch is much more pliable than hazel and, unlike willow, never roots itself. We cut suckering, well-branched stems during February or March. We place six or eight sticks in the ground – burying at least 22cm (9in) in the soil – to form a circle measuring 75cm (2½ft) in diameter. The rods splay outwards – like the ribs of a shuttlecock. Then we take two opposite pieces and bring them together to form a point, twisting the two stems together and then bending the ends back through the loop. We do this with all the opposite pairs, leaving all the twiggy branches on the inside to support the peas. The feathery side shoots are woven together like the rungs of a ladder. The whole structure is neatened up and the sweet pea seedlings are planted around the edge during March or April.

David Beaumont, Head Gardener at Hatfield House Park and Gardens, Hatfield, Hertfordshire

After the snowdrops have faded, it is time for the delicate wood anemones to flower. They only reveal themselves on bright days, staying tightly closed in bad weather. The wood anemones at Kingston Lacy have grown in the woods for hundreds of years and the garden is home to one of the National Collections, which contains 24 cultivars. Though they spread slowly, the regime described here will make them increase more readily.

We give our wood anemones (*Anemone nemorosa*) a dusting of bonemeal just before they appear every year and then we mulch them with bark every second year, just as they're dying down. When they become too congested – usually every fourth year – we divide them. They associate perfectly with deciduous ferns. The fern crosiers unfurl just after the anemones have finished flowering and so keep their roots cool. The perfect place for wood anemones is in a lightly shaded, but not too dry, site under deciduous trees. You can buy potted plants now or order dry rhizomes from a specialist bulb company during the autumn. 'Vestal' is a double white and 'Robinsoniana' a soft lilac; both are good doers.

Clive Cox, Senior Gardener at Kingston Lacy (The National Trust), Wimborne Minster, Dorset

It's possible to buy your snowdrops in March and April, when they're still in leaf. Known as 'in the green' snowdrops, these can be bought in large quantities for modest amounts. Choose forms of our native snowdrop *Galanthus nivalis* to begin with and then, if they grow well, progress to the more expensive and specialist bulbs, which are usually sold in smaller numbers.

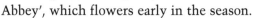 Now is the best time to order some *Galanthus nivalis* bulbs 'in the green'. These are dispatched in March and establish much more easily than dry bulbs planted in September. Our snowdrops enjoy growing in woodland, so position them under deciduous trees or shrubs. The single forms clump up better here than the doubles and we leave them to their own devices, dividing some every year. We intersperse them with winter aconites (*Eranthis hyemalis*). The single snowdrops and the aconites will self-seed. We also grow a vigorous, greener-leaved snowdrop called 'Anglesey Abbey', which flowers early in the season.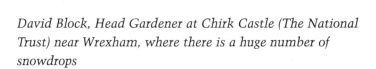

David Block, Head Gardener at Chirk Castle (The National Trust) near Wrexham, where there is a huge number of snowdrops

Snowdrops are the harbingers of spring, the first real flowers of the new gardening year. Yet few of us are blessed with the perfect soil or site for these virginal flowers. This advice will help you to establish a goodly number in your garden.

⮑ Choose a well-drained area in good light. Thoroughly prepare the ground by incorporating a good spade's depth of well-rotted manure before planting. Position the bulbs two or three times deeper than their height, spacing them 7cm (3in) apart. Add a sprinkle of bonemeal and surround them with some horticultural sharp sand before covering them. Water in well if your bulbs are in leaf. Preparation pays dividends and your snowdrops will increase much more readily.

Matt Bishop, Head Gardener of a private estate on the Hampshire/Dorset border and co-author of the sell-out monograph Snowdrops

Trilliums are more challenging than snowdrops or wood anemones, but this valuable advice should help us all.

When establishing trilliums buy living plants and not dried rhizomes as these rarely grow. Position them in deciduous shade or against a north-facing wall and, before planting, add lots of organic material to the soil. Making a raised bed in deep, rich soil is often more successful than growing them close to trees where it can be too dry. Trilliums can tolerate wet conditions during winter and spring and the secret is to keep them in leaf for as long as possible – at least to midsummer. This ensures that the food supply is replenished for next year's flowers.

Trilliums shouldn't be divided when dormant. They produce roots as they come into flower and May and June are the best times to divide them.

Nigel Rowland of Long Acre Plants near Wincanton, Somerset

High Beeches Garden, designed by Colonel Giles Loder, contains some spectacular magnolias and rare trees. Many were raised from seeds collected by Ernest 'Chinese' Wilson during the first years of the twentieth century.

New magnolias can take up to 20 years to flower, but feeding them with a handful of Growmore in late spring will make them flower more quickly. *Magnolia* x *soulangeana* is one of the easiest hybrids to grow, and flowers when young. It also flowers later in the season, thus tending to avoid frost damage. The evergreen *Magnolia grandiflora* is ideal against a sheltered wall and also produces flushes of flower through the summer even when young. Magnolias resent root disturbance. As well as conserving moisture, mulching with a 15cm (6in) layer of bark after flowering will suppress all annual weeds and avoid the need for any digging near the roots.

David Adams, Head Gardener at High Beeches, West Sussex

Exbury was established between the two World Wars by Lionel de Rothschild and remains in the de Rothschild family. It's particularly well-known for its acid-loving shrubs, which peak in May.

In early spring we mulch Exbury's famous rhododendrons with composted bracken (bought from the Forestry Commission). This suppresses weeds, keeps the roots cool and feeds them with trace elements. We also remove any dead wood on all shrubs and cut back the hydrangeas. The season here is extended by a large herbaceous garden that also contains late-season grasses, such as miscanthus, pennisetum and deschampsia. These have provided good winter seed heads, but now the plants must be cut back to the ground before the new shoots emerge.

*Rachel Martin,
Head Gardener
at Exbury
Gardens near
Southampton,
Hampshire*

Many National Collections are cared for by avid gardeners, but some are looked after by a local authority – a hangover from a time when young men and women were horticulturally trained in the Parks and Gardens department. Dudley Metropolitan Borough Council looks after the rudbeckia and ceanothus collections and Christine Morris is the enthusiast who keeps the show on the road.

Ceanothus grow wild in the chaparral, the Californian cowboy country where lots of old black and white westerns were shot. They're shallow-rooted, as they grow on dry scree slopes so it's a good idea to stake your plants, particularly when they're young. Give them a sunny and open position and you'll find them surprisingly hardy – as long as the ground is well-drained. Ceanothus have a tendency to flower themselves to death and die, usually when nine or 10 years old, and this happens quite suddenly and quickly. My two favourite evergreen varieties are 'Concha' and 'Italian Skies'. I also like the deciduous violet-blue 'Henry Desfosse'. Don't grow a ceanothus unless you really have the room: they are ruined if they're continually cut back and trimmed.

Christine Morris who helps to look after the National Collection of Ceanothus for Dudley Metropolitan Borough Council, West Midlands

Many gardeners favour mixed borders of shrubs and perennials and both of the following suggestions mingle really well with perennials.

The yellow foliage of the golden philadelphus (*Philadelphus coronarius* 'Aureus') scorches easily in sunlight, but if you cut it hard back during spring, this is prevented. We also do the same to our *Cotinus coggygria* 'Royal Purple' at the same time. Then it produces much larger leaves in a lovely shade of deep purple, rather than its own usual, rather duller, smaller leaves.

Ray Gibbs, Head Gardener at Parham House and Gardens near Pulborough, West Sussex

Here's another popular summer-flowering shrub that needs strict management at this time of the year.

Buddlejas are well worth growing in the garden as their nectar attracts over 20 species of butterfly – almost half our native population. The best time to prune your bushes is in early March. Cut back the old wood to two buds to encourage lots of new growth. If you have an old, overgrown buddleja, act on the side of caution and prune it in three stages, otherwise you might kill it. Cut back one third of the bush every year for three years – again in March. Any forms of *Buddleja davidii* can be pruned in this way.

Roger Sygraves, Head Gardener at Capel Manor College, Enfield, Middlesex

Pruning shears and secateurs to the ready – once the worst of the weather is over.

Cut back the Mediterranean plants – santolinas, lavenders, sages, cistus and artemisias – to the lowest buds. If you grow wisteria, look for the swollen buds and cut back to that point on each spur, removing any branches that are damaged or dying back. Some clematis (the Viticella and Jackmanii types) can also be cut back to the lowest fresh buds. Prune shrubs with coloured stems – cornus, willow and rubus – and ornamental grasses that have been left intact during winter, such as miscanthus, in mid-March.

Peter Kerley, Garden Supervisor at the University Botanic Gardens, Cambridge

After winter, one of the great gardening problems is judging whether or not that bare dead-looking shrub or tree is really turning up its toes or just resting until it bursts into leaf once again.

After winter, some evergreen shrubs may look dead and unsightly and there is a strong temptation to dig them out. Resist it! Instead, take a sharp knife and gently cut the bark to see if any green shows beneath, start just below the blackened leaves and, if the result is negative, try again lower down. If you find signs of green, then once spring seems here you can remove all the unsightly growth to encourage fresh leaves. If there are no signs of life after a few weeks give a gentle upwards pull to see if the roots are active. If there is no resistance, then and only then is the time to say farewell.

Robin Compton, owner of Newby Hall and Garden, Ripon, Yorkshire

Mediterranean plants such as lavender and sage have a tendency to get leggy and straggly. This system will prevent that woody look.

➤ When growing sages and lavenders, it's vital that you cut them back in the spring, after flowering, and again in September. This stops them from getting woody and diseased and keeps the new growth at the base of the plant. If you have your herbs in pots, remember to check them during September. Take hold of the foliage and lift the plant by the stem. If all is well, the plant should have a good solid, pot-shaped rootball. Once lifted, look at the roots. If there are any gaps or spaces in the rootball vine weevil may be present in the compost. Kill any grubs you find and in severe cases, destroy the plant.

Ted Riddell, owner of Cheshire Herbs near Tarporley, Cheshire (Gold Medal winners at Chelsea Flower Show)

Rosemary and lamb is one of the great spring combinations in the kitchen. Even if you're a vegetarian, rosemary is valuable for providing early flowers to sustain the emerging bees.

Spring is a good time to plant a rosemary bush in a sunny, free-draining place. If your soil is heavy, incorporate some coarse grit into it. There are blue, pink and white-flowered varieties in upright or prostrate forms. All are suitable for culinary use – don't be afraid to harvest the leaves as this keeps the plant bushy. The hotter and sunnier the site, the more aromatic the leaf. Existing bushes can also be tidied and clipped in spring. If too large, prune out the larger branches from the base. Cuttings can be taken between May and August.

Tim Upson, Superintendent of the University Botanic Garden, Cambridge

At Mottisfont Abbey, a garden famous for its old-fashioned roses, they want to delay their lavender flowers, so that they follow the main flush of roses.

To make our lavender bloom later, we cut the bushes hard back in mid-May. The first flowers will then appear in late July and are produced on and on through September and October. We have used 'Hidcote' and 'Munstead' widely in the past, but we're extending our range. Lavender can be easily raised from seed, but the plants do vary. It's better to raise your new plants from cuttings if you want to make a lavender hedge or line a pathway.

Clare Campbell, Gardener at Mottisfont Abbey (The National Trust) near Romsey, Hampshire

Some things are sent to try gardeners, and sowing parsnips can be one of the most aggravating pastimes as they are notoriously slow to germinate. After peering anxiously down at the soil for several weeks, the gardener often gives up hope and sows another row, and then another, until finally half the plot is covered in parsnips!

Parsnips are slow to germinate, taking at least 30 days. Mark the drill by oversowing the parsnips with radishes. By the time the radishes are ready, the parsnips will have germinated. A month before you want to sow the seeds of melons and courgettes, take them out of the packet and place them in your coat pocket. The grit will scar the seed coat making them germinate more easily.  When planting courgettes and cucumbers, place a carrot in the mound to attract harmful nematodes. When planting brassicas, place chopped up rhubarb leaves at the bottom of each hole to deter cabbage root fly.

Neil Porteous, Head Gardener at Clumber Park (The National Trust), Nottinghamshire

This is the perfect tip for gardeners who have a small garden where every inch counts.

My small garden is intensively planted and I always 'lift' the skirts on my shrubs by taking out the lower branches, so that I can utilize the ground right up to the main stems. I remove the lower branches only after the shrubs have been growing in the garden for two years. By then they are strong enough to withstand this treatment. I've found that the best time of year to prune is in late spring, when the sap is rising, as the cuts heal very quickly. The areas underneath the shrubs are planted with my favourite perennials – pulmonarias, phloxes and campanulas.

Sue Ward who gardens equally beautifully at Ladywood, Romsey, Hampshire

Gill Richardson's garden is famous for its snowdrops, but she also grows lots of other plants for year-round interest.

When choosing roses this spring, grow some that produce lovely hips. These look very decorative during the autumn and winter months and they attract birds into the garden. The flowers are usually single, but they are often attractively packed with stamens. Some of my favourites are 'Wickwar', a cream-flowered rambler with glaucous leaves, 'Francis E. Lester', with single flowers in apple-blossom pink that fades to white, *Rosa helenae*, a creamy white scrambler, 'Lykkefund', a creamy yellow rambler, and *R. rubrifolia*, a glaucous-leaved species with flagon-shaped hips.

*Gill
Richardson of
Manor Farm
in Keisby,
Lincolnshire*

Producing lovely roses isn't always easy and most gardeners have their own miracle feeds.

We feed all our roses with Epsom salts (magnesium sulphate) at the end of April, just as the leaves are appearing. It can be sprinkled on the soil or watered on with a can. This makes the rose healthier and helps to prevent diseases, especially black spot. We also use a foliar feed during the summer. Some roses are especially prone to black spot, but we find that rugosas never suffer and several other good roses are hardly ever affected, including the large shrub 'Cerise Bouquet', the smaller 'Queen of Denmark' ('Königin von Dänemark'), and the climbing 'Compassion'. Not all roses are susceptible, so if a rose is badly affected, try another. A thick mulch of manure in autumn helps to prevent black spot and always collect any diseased leaves that have fallen on to the ground.

Amanda Hornby of Hodges Barn near Tetbury, Gloucestershire

Tony Clear uses something else.

We feed our roses twice a year – in March and then again after the first flush of flowers – with a high potash rose fertilizer. This encourages more flowers and ripens the wood, making the rose hardier. The species and the groundcover roses are very disease resistant, so if you suffer badly from black spot grow some of these. *Rosa virginiana*, *R.* x *richardii*, *R. moyesii*, 'Harry Maasz' and the low growing 'Pheasant' also have wonderful orange and red hips. These endure through the winter, extending the season of interest to ten months of the year.

Tony Clear, Head Gardener at Brook Cottage in Alkerton near Banbury, Gloucestershire

Victorian gardeners were an innovative bunch and their gardening books describe how to grow a wide range of fruit and vegetables to supplement the larder. Charles Darwin's garden at Down House near Biggin Hill was his outdoor laboratory, as well as a source of fruit and vegetables for the kitchen. Nick Biddle urges us to be more inventive.

We use Charles Darwin's gardening books for inspiration and we've learnt that Victorian gardeners were much more adventurous than us. Books by Loudon and Thompson are full of information, ideas and techniques and are well worth reading during the winter months. One practical idea involves making simple cold frames (placed in a south-facing border or against a sheltered wall) and then sowing early vegetables like carrots, spinach, lettuce, beans and peas. A cold frame can be easily made using wood and plastic, or by building a temporary wall of bricks – it needn't be costly or permanent.

Nick Biddle, Garden Curator at Down House (English Heritage) near Biggin Hill, Kent

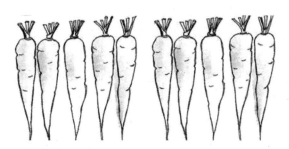

The most successful gardeners are sons of the soil, but whatever the condition of the soil there's still plenty to do. After reading this next piece of advice I can just picture Neil doing the soft-shoe shuffle along the rows.

When the soil sticks to your boots it's too wet to sow any seeds, but it's ideal for transplanting anything that needs moving or dividing. If the soil isn't sticking to your boots, it's perfect for sowing seeds. Use a length of string to mark the line, rake out the drill using a hoe and put the seed in the drill. Place your feet either side of the line and slowly shuffle along the row, keeping your feet on the ground. This action may look strange, but it covers the seeds – we call it shuffling in.

Neil Porteous, Head Gardener at Clumber Park (The National Trust), Nottinghamshire

This entertaining tip from Helen Dillon is about life rather than gardening. If only we assessed the risk factor before making our choices...

When choosing a dog for your garden, consider its sex and measure its legs: bitches make yellow puddle marks on the lawn and males do damaging squirts on the evergreens. But if you choose a he-dog with short legs, like a miniature dachshund, he lifts his leg with enthusiasm and invariably misses.

Helen Dillon who gardens beautifully at 45 Sandford Road, Dublin

As the weather warms up, your pets may begin scratching: your garden can provide the solution.

Hanging a bunch of herbs including lavender, pennyroyal, cotton lavender and rue above the kitchen door will repel summer flies. If your pets are scratching, sprinkle some rue in the dog's basket and some catmint and pennyroyal in the cat's basket to dicourage troublesome fleas. Finally, placing a vase of mixed mints on the kitchen windowsill freshens the air.

Tracey Pearman, Nursery Manager at Iden Croft Herbs, Staplehurst, Kent

Forget the first cuckoo, my favourite gardening noise is the sound of new potatoes hitting the bucket just after you've dug them up. My favourite culinary moment is eating some of them with lashings of butter. I shall certainly be trying this tip when I plant my next crop.

Chit your potatoes on a light window-sill. When you sow them at the end of March, rub out the weakest shoots, leaving the two strongest ones. Then nick the tuber with a sharp knife as you put it in the ground. This helps it to rot away quickly and then when you lift your new potatoes, you won't get a nasty smelly old potato in the middle of the roots. It also helps to deter the slugs.

Neil Porteous, Head Gardener at Clumber Park (The National Trust), Nottinghamshire

Here's another sound bit of advice on growing potatoes.

To clear the ground of wireworms, which damage potato crops, take some empty bean cans and puncture them, making several holes in the sides and bottom. Then fill the cans with potato peelings and bits of chopped potato and sink them into the ground. The wire worms will be attracted by the potato and can be removed and destroyed. When growing potatoes, choose a fast-maturing variety like 'Rocket' and get it in early, protecting the tops with a cloche. That way, the crop matures before the slugs can get going.

Julian Stanley, Head Gardener at the Ryton Organic Gardens (HDRA) near Coventry, Warwickshire

I always think of growing vegetables as the 'A' level of gardening. You can't just plant them and go away, you need to nurture and protect your charges from all manner of living things as they zoom in on your plot. Here's one way of staying on top.

When you sow a row of peas during early spring the mice will eat half of them and sometimes more, because they can smell the seeds. If you sow your peas and top-dress them with pelleted poultry manure, they never find them.

Lesley Rootham, Head Gardener at The Old Rectory, Burghfield, Berkshire

This rhyme sums it up. Geoff Hillman, a wonderful gardener, was once watching me sow some peas and came out with it. He learnt it as a boy some 80 years ago.

 One for the mouse
One for the crow
One to rot
And one to grow.

Geoff Hillman of The Old Surgery in Hook Norton, Oxfordshire

Hill Top used to belong to Beatrix Potter. The gardener there, Peter Tasker, relies on his pot marigolds for plant protection.

One of the favourite plants we grow at Hill Top is the humble pot marigold (*Calendula officinalis*). This cottage garden favourite is getting harder to find in its original, uncorrupted form but it is well worth searching out. Seed is sown in March in the greenhouse and the young plants are set out in the garden in April. From early summer until often as late as Christmas, the plants produce a profusion of cheerful orange blooms and, if grown in among vegetables, will attract beneficial insects such as hoverflies, the larvae of which happily munch their way through hundreds of greenfly in a season.

Peter Tasker of Hill Top (The National Trust) near Ambleside, Cumbria

Gardening on heavy soil can be a frustrating experience. Working the soil too early in the year can wreak havoc on its structure.

From the moment the garden at Great Dixter closes for the season at the end of October, we're busy on the borders to get them ready for reopening the following April. There's precious little time to lose – so we have to get on the ground even when it's wet. Our heavy clay soil makes this even harder, so we make sure that we add plenty of organic matter and 3–5mm washed horticultural grit as soil conditioners. A healthy soil with a good structure will stand more abuse than unimproved soil. And even though the compost eventually rots away, the grit stays put helping the drainage and making future cultivation so much easier.

Fergus Garrett, Head Gardener at Great Dixter, East Sussex

Fergus walks the plank at Great Dixter – in the interests of preserving the soil. In fact a scaffolding plank could be a great Christmas gift for the gardener, but it's a bit difficult to wrap!

Standing directly on our heavy clay soils during wet weather means that we could easily ruin our soil structure. Working off shortened scaffolding boards and bits of ply board means that our weight is distributed preventing the soil from getting compacted (as well as giving us a cosier surface to work from rather than the cold paving or wet soil). Sometimes we use a system of planks weaving them in between plants. The boards are scraped clean regulary as we work, and all the preparation work is done before we dig. The last thing we want to do is open up the soil and then leave it to take in all the rain. Using a fork rather than a spade helps as there is less 'smearing', and the planting is done immediately after digging. We don't mulch after planting at Dixter as we want all our self-sowers such as poppies, red orach, verbenas, to come up and provide the 'linking element' through our borders.

Fergus Garrett, Head Gardener at Great Dixter, East Sussex

Heavy soil also afflicts Denmans and here they use gravel to grow a wider range of plants.

We have a dry river bed, made from gravel and pebbles, running through the centre of the garden. This area is very natural and the plants – verbascums, sea hollies and foxgloves – are encouraged to seed down. We do have to thin them out, but this random planting, which also contains miscanthus, carex and bamboo, looks very effective and natural. Having a well-drained, gravelled or pebbled area allows plants to self-seed much more freely. The gravel protects the seeds until they're ready to germinate and stops of crowns of established plants from rotting off. Gardeners, particularly those on heavy soil, could use this material in any open part of the garden to grow eryngiums, grey-leaved euphorbias and verbenas.

Andrew Muggeridge, Head Gardener at Denmans near Arundel, West Sussex

While some of your shrubs may still be in limbo, your summer-flowering perennials are likely to be growing apace. Professional gardeners increase their stock by taking Irishman's cuttings, which will soon turn into more plants.

Spring is the ideal time to increase your stocks of perennials. Look for shoots about 5cm (2in) in length and take them as cuttings using a sharp knife. Remove the shoot at root level to include a portion of root at the base of each cutting. Pot these up individually in small pots in a mixture of 70 per cent compost to 30 per cent vermiculite. Place them in a cold frame in a sheltered spot or in an unheated greenhouse and they will root within 10 days. Once they are rooted repot each cutting in a larger pot of compost. Many plants can be quickly increased in this way, including pulmonarias, delphiniums, dahlias and chrysanthemums.

Paul Cook, Head Gardener at Arley Hall and Gardens, Northwich, Cheshire

If you didn't or couldn't divide your plants during the autumn you can get busy now.

When stripping and replanting an area of garden, work on a piece about 10m (30ft) square and lift all the plants and remove any perennial weeds. Thickly mulch the whole area with compost or well-rotted manure and turn it straight into the soil. Divide the plants, dig the necessary holes – adding a handful of bonemeal to the bottom of each – and replant the divisions. Then re-mulch the whole area. This will give your plants an excellent start and keep the soil in good heart.

Ray Gibbs, Head Gardener at Parham House and Gardens near Pulborough, West Sussex

The garden at Pensthorpe Wildfowl Park and Garden was a millennium project commissioned by the owner. It peaks in late summer and was designed by Piet Oudolf, using 12,500 plants. As well as being attractive in itself, this late summer spectacle has some special plus points.

A garden that attracts lots of butterflies, insects and birds is a delight, and this is one of the big advantages of a prairie-style planting. It involves using large drifts of late-flowering plants and grasses in blocks of 20 or 30, creating a natural look. For a site that is set into a wild or rural landscape the biggest advantage of this sort of planting is that it blends into the landscape beyond, making the garden appear much larger. We cut down any of the plants that go soggy – the persicarias, for instance – and those that could seed a little too efficiently – the echinops – but most of the seed heads are left intact until February.

Bill Makins, Director of the Pensthorpe Waterfowl Park, Garden and Nature Reserve near Fakenham, Norfolk

Most gardeners can only dream of owning a walled garden – the one at Chatsworth covers 3½ acres (1.5 hectares).

We make successive sowings of many crops straight into the ground. We sow them as thinly as possible. If the weather is dry when they need thinning, we water the line of seedlings thoroughly with a can beforehand. After thinning we water the row again to limit the disturbance at the root. We also prefer to lightly thin our rows twice, once early on and once later. We harvest our carrots when they're very young, about the size of a little finger. The maincrop carrots are sown at the end of June, when the crop is less likely to be attacked by carrot root fly.

Ian Webster, Head Gardener at Chatsworth near Bakewell, Derbyshire

Thinning out annuals
Water seedlings the night before...
...roots are easier to pull out next day

One of the most popular plants is the clematis and, well grown, they make a significant addition to any garden. These members of the Ranunculeae, named after Rana, the frog, demand a cool, moist root run. This isn't always easy on the drier, eastern side of the country, but here's one solution.

When planting clematis, begin by soaking the pot in a bucket of water and then dig a hole about 60cm (2ft) from the wall. Tease out the roots (a good practice with any plant) and place the rootball in the hole, angling the plant towards the wall. Clematis need shade at their base, so partly cover the roots with soil and then place a piece of stone or paving (15cm² (6in sq)) on top, covering it with soil. Water in well. The stone keeps the roots cool. Always try to plant a clematis in tandem with another climber.

Martin Duncan one of the two Head Gardeners at Audley End (English Heritage), Saffron Walden, Essex

When dry weather strikes some clematis suffer with wilt, which turns them into a drooping, dying plant within days.

Clematis wilt can be a problem with large-flowered clematis. Planting these 6–7cm (2½–3in) below the soil surface will help to prevent it, enabling the plant to build up a better root system. Many gardeners blame clematis wilt when their plants are looking dry and brown at the base. This is lack of water and not true wilt. To avoid the problem of dryness, water your spring- and summer-planted clematis every other day for the first three to four months of their lives. The very best time to plant clematis is during September, when the soil is still warm and usually moist.

Raymond Evison of Guernsey Clematis Nursery, Guernsey

Tulips add a real touch of elegance to every garden and this tip from Hugh Johnson should ensure a tasteful display.

In a colour-themed border or bed, start the year with tulips of the same colour, to state the theme with trumpets: yellow tulips can be used in predominately yellow borders and so on. This type of planting is brilliantly successful at Hadspen House in Somerset. There are plenty of colours and forms to choose from: lily-flowered 'White Triumphator' (a clear white), 'West Point' (an elegant and yellow) and 'Dyanito' (a red and yellow) can be used *en masse*, as can the dark maroon 'Queen of Night', the pale pink, fringed 'Bellflower', and the completely red 'Prominence'. Other tulips of the same type and similar colour can be blended in. The dark tulips could be a forerunner to equally sultry summer flowers – dark astrantias, *Anthriscus sylvestris* 'Raven's Wing' and the rose 'Charles de Mills', for instance.

Hugh Johnson of Saling Hall near Braintree, Essex

Next comes some very sound advice from Chenies in Buckinghamshire, where the tulips are always stunning.

Fireblight can be a problem with tulips. Affected plants have warped and twisted flowers. Following this regime helps to prevent it. After flowering, snap off the flower-heads to prevent the petals from falling on to the ground. Take the stems down to 5–7cm (2–3in), which, with the two leaves, looks attractive. Invest in new tulip bulbs every year, thoroughly clearing the old ones from the soil. We start to lift our tulips on the 18 May. Don't plant your tulips until late November or early December. Add a generous layer of compost after planting. If fireblight occurs, dig out the infected soil and replace it.

Elizabeth MacLeod Matthews of The Manor House, Chenies, Buckinghamshire

After the tulips fade, you'll need to replace them.

Penstemons are the perfect plants to replace spent tulips. We use 'Evelyn', 'Garnet', 'Sour Grapes' and 'Burford Seedling' for late summer colour. It's possible to take penstemon cuttings throughout the year – using the new side-shoots – so it's easy to raise new plants. The best way to preserve your penstemons in the border is to keep all the top growth intact through the winter, cutting it back hard in late April. We also grow many deutzias, which are very hardy and flower well as long as you're drastic and remove three quarters of the old wood after flowering.

Anne and John Chambers, owners of Kiftsgate Court, Gloucestershire

As soon as spring really gets going the lawn needs mowing. At Yalding the grass looks green and fit, and it is all done without chemicals.

Eighty per cent of the gardening chemicals sold are applied to lawns, but you can have a well-fed, healthy lawn without them. Instead of removing the clippings week after week, which robs the lawn of nutrients, we advocate setting the blades on the mower slightly higher and leaving the grass box off. Allow the clippings to lie on the lawn after mowing and they will add fertility to the soil as they rot down. The web of life under the grass pulls the material down through the soil, so there isn't a build up of thatch. You'll end up with a healthier lawn. If you've got some clover so much the better, it also adds fertility.

Nick Robinson, Head Gardener at Yalding Gardens (HDRA) near Maidstone, Kent

Standen near East Grinstead is a very Edwardian, very English house with William Morris connections. On long summer afternoons, a game of croquet would be the perfect thing.

The croquet lawn is aerated once a week during spring to allow the water to drain away. This prevents moss forming and allows the grass to develop deeper roots, ensuring that it looks good during hot, dry weather. However small your lawn, thoroughly aerating it, scarifying it (removing the thatch with a lawn rake) and then applying a high nitrogen feed will pay dividends later in the year. We have another lawn that we treat very differently. It's cut on a high setting and only given a low nitrogen fertilizer – this allows wildflowers to flourish.

James Masters, Gardener-in-Charge at Standen (The National Trust) near East Grinstead, West Sussex

Low-lying gardens can have problems and this idea, from Dave Roberts of Rufford Old Hall, should help with water-logged soil.

Parts of this garden are only 6m (20ft) above sea level and are very damp. We grow the plants that thrive in such conditions – hostas, astilbes, rheums, gunneras and bergenias – and we always plant during spring. One of the easiest ways to improve the drainage in a damp corner is to mound up the soil above the height of the lawn or path, so that the water can drain away. Adding gravel or broken bricks before mounding up also helps. We lightly mulch these areas with friable leaf mould. The frogs, toads and ducks obligingly clear away our slugs.

Dave Roberts, Gardener-in-Charge at Rufford Old Hall (The National Trust) near Ormskirk, Lancashire

Whether you want to create a wild pond, or have formal fountains like a mini-Versailles, there are sensible rules about what you should (and shouldn't) grow.

☞ The best time to restock your pond or divide your existing aquatic plants is at the beginning of the season. By early April the water should be warming up and new plants will have a whole season to establish themselves. The general rule of thumb when stocking a new pond is to use one oxygenator for every 60cm (2ft) square of pond, and one waterlily for every 8m (25ft) square. Floating plants and oxygenators are vital, but marginal plants are not as necessary for a healthy pond. It just looks better. Waterlilies usually need dividing between the second and fifth year. They also benefit from aquatic fertilizer tablets to stimulate growth.

Mat Hughes of the Stapely Water Gardens near Nantwich, Cheshire

When spring finally slides into summer and the fear of frost is over, a whole new range of possibilities opens up.

Release your house plants into the garden. Bromeliads, sparrmannias and tradescantias are no less hardy than pelargoniums and petunias. They will all grow really well in dappled shade, making your garden look really exotic. The Victorians used to plant out coleus (now known as solenostemon) in massive bedding schemes. New plants can be bought in spring and planted out into the soil in blocks and by September they'll have made large plants. There are golds, reds and dark blacks. Cuttings are easily rooted, just place short lengths in water. The trick is to pinch the flowers out, leaving the dazzling leaves.

Will Giles of the Exotic Garden in Thorpe, Norwich, Norfolk

I'm not sure whether this is for the benefit of the seeds or the gardener, but it conjures up a lovely picture and proves that we gardeners are a sensuous lot.

Because of lower light levels and the lack of any breeze, seedlings grown in the greenhouse are often taller and weaker than those grown outside. To toughen them up, brush them gently 10 to 20 times each day with your hand or a piece of card. This will make the seedlings stockier and more able to withstand the rigours of life when planted out in the garden. Like some gardeners, seedlings seem to respond better when stroked in the morning!

Peter Tasker, Head Gardener at Hill Top (The National Trust) near Ambleside, Cumbria

This is one of the most useful garden tips for growing plants or seedlings.

If you grow your own bedding plants, use a loam-based compost rather than a peat-based one as peat-based composts are impossible to rehydrate once they've dried out. Once you've potted up your plants in loamy compost, water them heavily for the first two days and then reduce the watering. This encourages the roots to search out the water (now at the bottom of the pot) by putting down deep roots. When the plant reaches the sides of the pot, it is ready to go outside. Prepare your bed well by double digging and adding manure to form an open, friable mixture. Add sand and John Innes No.3 compost to heavy soils.

Frank Parge, Gardener-in-Charge at Hughenden Manor (The National Trust) near High Wycombe, Buckinghamshire

This simple preparation during spring will stop your borders from flagging later in the year.

It's no good waiting until the plant is wilting or losing leaves before you water it, by then the root hairs will have suffered and the plant will be thoroughly stressed. Set up an irrigation system in early spring. Top-dress the border with blood, fish and bone, lay a seep hose down and cover it with a thick layer of well-rotted manure, leaf mould or garden compost. Apply the mulch when the ground is saturated, not over dry soil. After a week without rain, use the seep hose for several hours during the evening or over-night. This system is much better than using a sprinkler, which does more harm than good.

Randal Anderson, Head Gardener at Daylesford House near Stow-on-the-Wold, Gloucestershire

Summer

There's a moment of warm softness that defines the start of summer. And where spring is often a frustrating series of false starts, forcing every gardener to play the waiting game, with summer, suddenly, it's full steam ahead. The grass will sometimes need mowing twice a week, the vegetable plot will need almost daily attention and the greenhouse will constantly beckon, but the prospect of many a long evening in the garden is ahead of us. In all, there's an optimistic anticipation of pleasures yet to come.

For those admirers of striped lawns, mowed to perfection, this ever-so-simple tip will allow you to cut the neatest, straightest sward through the grass.

If you want to get bold stripes on your lawn, you will need a good, heavy cylinder mower. Once you're equipped, the trick is to look at where the sun is before you start mowing. It will cast a shadow of the mower on to the lawn as you move along. This shadow will make it difficult to see the grass clearly, so you need to ensure that it falls on the parts of the lawn you've already cut. This leaves the grass you're cutting in full sun, allowing you to get a very neat edge as you go up and down.

Bill Boardman, owner of The Garden in an Orchard, Burgh Apton near Norwich, Norfolk

It's reassuring to know that head gardeners also have to struggle with weeds, including that most difficult underground traveller – bindweed. There are no easy solutions for dealing with this climbing pest, but Stephen Cooling, who looks after 7 acres (3 hectares) of garden, believes in swift action.

We do have some bindweed in the garden and the best way to tackle it is to catch it early when about 2.5cm (1in) of growth is showing. Spray the shoots with glyphosate and then spray about a month later. If you persist and spray every 3 or 4 weeks (catching the young growth each time) the bindweed will disappear. Spraying just once isn't effective, though. Perennial weeds need to be worried continuously.

Stephen Cooling, Gardener-in-Charge at Clandon Park near Guildford, Surrey

In a crowded border, spraying weeds with glyphosate isn't always an option, but this system of targeting individual shoots is another practical way of dealing with the problem.

One of the hardest weeds to eradicate is bindweed. It's impossible to dig every bit of it out and in many older gardens it goes underneath established shrubs and roses. As the new growth emerges, put on rubber gloves and rub the leaves with a weed stick designed to kill dandelions. Looking rather like a wax candle, this causes the shoot to die back, killing the root. Another way is to angle bamboo canes into the ground and allow the bindweed to weave its way along them, away from the plant. Then you can spray with glyphosate.

David Kempson, Head Gardener at Belvoir Castle,
Leicestershire

The biggest problem in my Cotswold garden has always been lack of rainfall, but further north, in Lancashire, they've got more than enough – and it's cold. Some plants love copious amounts of rain, but the silver-leaved Mediterranean sun-lovers need careful nurturing.

I always plant Mediterranean and silver-leaved plants in gravel and add coarse grit beforehand to ensure that the border is well-drained. I edge my beds with stone, but I drill holes in the gaps along the edging to allow water to escape. I clip the lavender flowers off in autumn, but because of our harsh weather, I wait until late spring before cutting the lavender bushes hard back. I also clip the santolinas into a good, round shape just after the last frost, usually in June. This stops them from flopping and encourages silvery new growth.

Arabella Lennox-Boyd, garden designer and co-owner of Gresgarth Hall, Lancashire

Gardeners are always encouraged to enrich their soil with organic matter, but many plants will thrive on lighter, thinner soils. Aromatic plants and herbs adore the sandy soil at Felbrigg Hall where lavenders, sages, origanums and thymes are planted to lure in those important pollinators, the bees. The cardoons in this walled garden add real presence, but these sumptuous plants need feeding. Mulch with well-rotted manure during spring.

Herbs love growing in sunny positions and poor soil. Ours thrive in south-facing borders and are never fed. The cardoons at the back of the border are restricted to two flowering stems, which we stake with tree ties. The cardoon flowers are harvested, blanched and eaten when they are small. We also grow angelica and a host of other herbs that we allow to flower. The invasive herbs, like mint and horseradish, are kept in large pots and are repotted every second year. Herbs can't be sprayed, so you must remove any diseased or affected shoots as soon as you spot them.

Mark Hiorns-Neale, herb gardener at Felbrigg Hall (The National Trust) near Cromer, Norfolk

Learning to recognize and appreciate foliage colour, which varies from dark green through to silver-white, is an essential part of planning a border, and the best gardens use foliage widely as a foil to the flowers. An ill-considered collection of greens jars the eye in the same way that a flower-packed jumble of every colour in the rainbow is not as pleasing as a careful selection. This sound advice comes from Barrington Court, a garden with colour-themed borders that really work.

We are careful in the way we use colour, creating three distinct schemes. In the white garden we found that combining silver-leaved plants with white flowers just didn't work. Green leaves and touches of variegated foliage in silver and white hold this cool scheme together well, but not cream and white. In the hot borders we use oranges, yellows and sunny reds adding the dark leaves of the castor-oil plant (*Ricinus gibsonii*), dark-leaved cannas, ornamental beet and perilla to add drama. The mixed colour borders feature pinks and deep purples, which we combine with silver leaves. The most difficult colours to place are cool blue-pinks and blue-reds.

Christine Brain at Barrington Court (The National Trust), Somerset

Once you've decided on your colour scheme, it's time to get busy and do some planting. This planting tip will make your garden flow naturally, maximizing the effect.

May is a big time for planting new perennials in a border. Gaps need filling where there have been winter casualties or where things have been moved or divided. Where space permits we always plant in threes and fives. When we use five perennials, we don't plant them in a block, we put three together to make a triangle. Then we set out the other two plants individually away from the group of three, making sure all five are visible at once. This makes the drift look larger, creating the illusion that there are more plants in the border and giving it a natural feel.

Sally Briggs,
Head Gardener
at Merriments
Gardens in
Sussex

Some gardeners (and I have to confess I'm one) just can't resist the lure of growing as many different plants as they can shoehorn in; Mark Robson has learnt how to turn a plantsman's garden into a thing of beauty.

We like to grow lots of different plants and we may grow 10 or 11 different varieties of the same thing in one area. To make the border look more natural and unite the planting, we use several grasses that we repeat throughout the garden. *Stipa gigantea*, a tall, airy oat grass, fountains out over the shorter plants. *Stipa arundinacea*, a shorter later-flowering grass, is another favourite. These grasses last for months in the border. We plant very densely and one of our other tricks is to weed meticulously in the first 45–60cm (18–24in) of the beds closest to the edge of the lawn or path. By maintaining these edges we give the impression that the entire garden is perfectly maintained.

Mark Robson, Bide-a-Wee Cottage Garden, Stanton, near Morpeth, Northumberland

Tulips mix well with herbaceous plants, particularly late-flowering perennials. Some gardeners leave them in, but replacing them every year guarantees you first-rate flowers and gives you the room for summer bedding.

We are known for our tulips and we leave gaps between all our herbaceous plants in order to accommodate them. When the tulips are over, we replace them with dahlias. We recommend spraying dahlias with a fungicide and insect killer every two weeks from May or June. This prevents leaf spot and capsid bugs – two particular enemies. The dahlias are planted in blocks and staked with short sturdy stakes when they go out. As they grow taller, narrower stakes are used. 'Fascination', a tall and pale amethyst, and 'Berlin', a pink pompon, are two favourites here.

Elizabeth MacLeod Matthews of The Manor House, Chenies, Buckinghamshire

This planting scheme uses tulips, but this time with roses – another winning combination. Classically shaped tulips can also be used in box parterres, but they will need to be lifted every year.

We grow tulips and roses together. It's a simple scheme that works well. The tulips flower in April and May and then the roses carry on from June to October and the manure mulch feeds both. Many of our tulips have been in the garden for 15 years. We can't replant year after year or dig them up after flowering, but the following technique keeps them tidy and helps them flower the next year. As soon as the petals fall, the tulips are cut down to one leaf. The roses soon take over the display, while the tulip bulb is replenished for next year.

Anthony O'Grady, Head Gardener at Penshurst Place near Tonbridge, Kent

You can almost see the garden growing during the early part of summer and it's the perfect time to capitalize and increase your stock of perennial plants and dahlias. At Great Dixter, where they like to keep the borders looking fresh for their garden visitors, they plan ahead.

Keeping the garden looking fresh late into September/ October is always a challenge. Basal shoot cuttings, taken from dahlias, Michaelmas daisies, perennial helianthus and heleniums in May and put into John Innes cuttings compost, will root quickly and be ready to plant out in July. These will flower much later than normal and give us the freshness and late burst of colour that we so need at the end of Summer. Deadheading is essential for keeping things looking fresh. Self-sown teasels turning brown at the same time as the borders are still in flower, can drag a garden into an autumnal appearance prematurely. We thin these out only leaving a few in the best places so that we can appreciate their winter skeletons.

Fergus Garrett, Head Gardener at Great Dixter, East Sussex

Moisture-loving plants tend to flower from midsummer onwards and few are as dramatic as the gunnera, that huge-leaved rhubarb look-alike. This tip from Home Covert makes the leaves even larger.

Our garden is fed by streams that form the basis of the River Avon and we grow many waterside plants. One of our most handsome is the gunnera with its huge leaves. We have found that removing the conical flower spikes at this time of year allows the plant to concentrate its energy into producing bigger and bolder leaves, rather than producing seeds. However, we do allow some plants to self-seed, the bog primulas and the skunk cabbages, for instance. This is a good time to divide moisture-loving perennials such as ligularias; large clumps of bog primulas should be divided after flowering.

John Phillips of Home Covert, Roundway near Devizes, Wiltshire

The third week in May brings the Chelsea Flower Show, when gardeners descend on the Royal Hospital to marvel at the floral pavilions and ogle at the show gardens. This gardening tip comes from the owner of one of the finest small gardens in England. A perfectly planted, feminine garden, relying on pastel-coloured cottage garden plants, it is hidden behind a modern, detached house. The whole garden is set under a dappled canopy of mature birches.

I give some of my herbaceous plants the 'Chelsea chop', which means I reduce the main stems by a third in mid-May. This produces a better crop of flowers on many varieties: *Anthemis* 'E.C. Buxton' is a good example, but you can do it with delphiniums and all sorts of perennials. *Phlox paniculata* is a trademark plant in this garden and in order to lengthen the flowering season, I reduce one third of the stems by half, selecting those at the back of the clump, during May. As the first stems flower, the back stems (the ones I shortened) take over and every bloom is deadheaded as it fades. This system gives three flushes of flower.

Sue Ward of 53 Ladywood, Eastleigh, Hampshire (open under The National Gardens Scheme)

The Reverend Pemberton bred 32 fragrant roses and called them the hybrid musks. Of those, at least a dozen are classic garden roses. They're floriferous and free of disease and they have an old-fashioned, arching shape. Campanulas, in soft pinks and blues, are perfect partners to them, beginning to flower a few weeks before the roses.

I grow campanulas among my hybrid musk roses. The campanulas flower in June and varieties like *C. lactiflora* 'Loddon Anna' and *C. lactiflora* 'Prichard's Variety' can reach 1.5m (5ft) and be quite thuggish. After flowering, the campanulas are chopped down to a height of 60cm (24in) or just a bit less and this encourages new side shoots. These new shoots flower in late July and August when the hybrid musk roses ('Penelope', 'Cornelia', 'Felicia' and 'Buff Beauty') are at their peak. I also do this with monardas, alstroemerias, cirsium and anthemis to encourage a second flush of flowers in other areas of the garden.

Xa Tollemache, a garden designer who gardens at Helmingham Hall, Suffolk

Rambling roses have romantic castle walls to climb at Crathes, but some are left to tumble gracefully downwards.

The high stone walls and steep rocky banks of Crathes Castle support many roses. After flowering, the rambling roses, which flower only once, have their long, new growths reduced by a third. This encourages new sideshoots resulting in more flowers of a better quality for next year. Some of our climbing and rambling roses are planted at the top of steep walls and banks and allowed to cascade downwards, mimicking their growth in the wild. The clear light of northern Scotland intensifies flower colour and we direct sow blue annuals – convolvulus, echiums, anchusas and nemophila – in the box parterre during the second week of May, after we've trimmed the box.

Callum Pirnie, Head Gardener at Crathes Castle, Aberdeenshire

The heart of Coughton Court is the Labyrinth Garden – an area that relies heavily on old-fashioned roses and cottage garden flowers. The straight paths follow a maze-like pattern and the maintenance regime is intense to keep the area at the peak of perfection. As many roses are close to the paths and arches where people pass, the more vigorous among them have to be restrained and pruned, and the pruning is more radical than at Crathes.

Rambling roses flower prolifically once, usually in early summer. When they've finished flowering, we remove the old flowering stems from the base and train in the new growths, leaving the new stems intact. We also give the plant a good feed with a rose fertilizer to promote strong growth. The stems begin to shed their leaves in October, but the wood is still supple enough to bend. We space the stems out and tie them in securely using garden twine. My two favourites are 'Sander's White Rambler', a late-flowering pure white with rich green leaves, and 'Debutante', a pale pink.

David Whitehead, Head Gardener at Coughton Court near Alcester, Warwickshire

79

One of the tricks of training roses is to slow down the rising sap. The result is more flowers and there are various ways of achieving this. Stems can be wound around rustic poles, or made to dip and bend below their natural level. At Alnwick they go one step further.

Old-fashioned and shrub roses have made plenty of growth by August and September. We peg down all these new leaders to hazel stakes to form a shape a little like an octopus with tentacles – we take the branches down as low as we can. The idea of gently bending the branches down is to put the sap under pressure and prevent it from simply going to the top end of each leader. This slows its movement and encourages each bud along its length to form a short flowering spur. By next summer the stems are studded with masses of roses, not just a few on the top.

Chris Gough, Head Gardener at Alnwick Gardens, Northumberland

Growing roses needn't involve using lots of chemicals. The hands-on approach described here works well in every garden. It is also worth remembering that some roses are very disease-resistant.

We are going organic at Llanerchaeron so we can't use toxins in the garden. We watch our roses very carefully and pick off any leaves that have black spot before they hit the ground. Each leaf has thousands of spores and we are very vigilant. Part of disease prevention is to take out any diseased or dying branches to allow air to flow through the bushes. We also mulch the roses with farmyard manure to prevent powdery mildew, which is a water-stress disease. We constantly rub away greenfly or wash them off with a mild detergent, nipping any trouble in the bud.

Patricia Griffiths, Gardener at Llanerchaeron (The National Trust), Aberaeron near Ceredigion, Wales

Companion planting is an ancient art, described by Pliny the Elder in his *Historia Naturalis*, written in the first century AD. He recorded which plants were beneficial when grown with grapes and his predecessor, Virgil, also mentions the art of combining flowers and vegetables. It actually does work and, where vegetable crops are concerned, it's obviously healthier not to use sprays and to rely on natural remedies, instead.

Always plant pot marigolds (calendulas) close to root crops. They secrete chemicals underground that repel pests. Add some pungent-leaved French marigolds to keep aphids away from your crops. Cabbage White butterflies, which strip brassicas, prefer to lay their eggs on nasturtiums, so edge your plot with these. Mask the smell of carrots by planting onions either side of your rows. If a cabbage should succumb to cabbage root fly (displaying purple-edged leaves and stunted growth) leave it in the ground. Pulling it up will make the grubs move to another cabbage.

Tina Hammond, Head Gardener at Felbrigg Hall (The National Trust), Norfolk

Being too impatient and sowing plants too early can lead to all sorts of gardening disasters. For example, it's important that French and runner beans are not subjected to the cold nights of early May. In Oxfordshire, the traditional day for the first sowing is 13 May, but the experienced gardener makes successive sowings over many weeks.

Early June is a good time for runner beans, climbing French beans and dwarf French beans to be sown straight into the soil. Use wigwams made from four canes to support the climbing varieties, planting two seeds per cane. Protect the young plants from strong winds. Making a mini cloche with half a plastic bottle works well. We sow climbing beans just once, but dwarf French beans are sown in drills every few weeks throughout the summer. They all make decorative flowering plants and the pods of French beans can be golden, purple and splashed black, as well as green.

Sarah Wain, Head Gardener at West Dean Gardens near Chichester, West Sussex

Box hedging was an integral part of every large garden. Although this tough plant is very hardy, late frosts can reduce the new growth to a dead, brown mess. Early June was always considered the best time for trimming and the perfect opportunity arose during Royal Ascot when the whole family was away at the races. Derby Day is still an important reminder to head gardeners to trim the box parterre.

This is the best time of year to trim box hedges and we use traditional lawn clippers regularly sharpened with emery cloth to enable us to keep our hedges 20cm (8in) high and 20cm (8in) deep. The two varieties of box we grow are the green *Buxus sempervirens* 'Suffruticosa' and the gold-tipped *B. sempervirens* 'Notata'. Before cutting, set out a straight line with red baler twine (which can be easily seen) to the desired height. Then lay out long strips of heavy duty plastic underneath the hedge to make the trimmings easy to collect. After cutting, fold the plastic strips carefully and tip the cuttings straight into the barrow. Careful preparation is the key to success.

Neil Cook, Head Gardener at Hanbury Hall (The National Trust) near Droitwich, Worcestershire

The walled garden and the orchard provided all the food for the household. Apples and pears were particularly important as many varieties could be stored for future use. The skilful job of pruning and thinning produced the necessary flower buds. Fruit trees, now available on dwarf rootstocks, are becoming an integral part of people's gardens once again. This tip will produce better fruit.

If you grow apples and pears it's very important that the fruits are thoroughly thinned. Wait for the June drop, when the tree sheds all its unwanted fruit, and then get busy. Leave one fruit per cluster, aiming for a 15cm (6in) gap between apples and a 10cm (4in) gap between pears. Although this seems ruthless, it will give you large, well-formed fruit. If you're thinking of growing apples for the first time, cordons are the most straightforward plant for beginners. Go to a specialist nursery and research which varieties you need to grow together for pollination purposes.

Jim Buckland, Head Gardener at West Dean Gardens near Chichester, West Sussex

Many estate gardens had huge greenhouses against their south-facing walls. Wallington has one of the most spectacular runs of glass in any walled garden. The Victorian peach house and the Edwardian conservatory are packed full of tender plants as well as fruit. The older varieties of pelargoniums were used as cut flowers for the house during the winter.

Modern pelargoniums tend to be very compact, but some of the old-fashioned cultivars are naturally vigorous and leggy and can be trained to cover a sunny conservatory or greenhouse wall. 'Duke of Buckingham' (orange-red), 'Melva Bird' (dark red) and 'Royal Purple' (syn. 'Brook's Purple') will easily reach 2m (6ft) in height. Tie in the shoots to a wall tie or trellis and feed regularly with a phosphate-rich tomato feed, deadheading regularly through the summer. Summer is also a good time to 'top and tail' potted plants by removing the compost from the bottom of the roots and replacing it with John Innes No.3 to boost new growth.

John Ellis, Head Gardener of Wallington (The National Trust) near Morpeth, Northumberland

Don't despair if you can't run to a Victorian peach house. There's still plenty of scope for growing some exotic plants in your garden. To succeed with some of the easier salvias, you don't need a sun-drenched south wall either – just incorporate some grit or rubble into the soil.

The key to overwintering salvias is to provide them with excellent drainage. Forms of *Salvia greggii*, *S. microphylla* and the hybrid between them, *S.* x *jamensis*, are the easiest to overwinter. They come in a variety of colours and provide flowers from June until November. These three are hardy to –10°C (14°F). Choose a sunny site (sheltered from strong winds) and plant them in the ground by late August. Deadhead as and when the flowers fade and then leave the top growth intact over winter. Cut back hard during late May or June and take cuttings from the resultant new growth.

William Dyson, Curator of Great Comp Garden and owner of Dyson's Nurseries near Sevenoaks, Kent

Always take cuttings of any tender or silver-leaved plant as an insurance policy against the devastatingly wet or cold winter that inevitably occurs every few years or so. The potash dressing described below can be used on hardy fuchsias, ceanothus and many other plants from warmer climes.

From midsummer onwards we take cuttings from the tender plants in the gardens, including the fuchsias, salvias and argyranthemums. We put several cuttings in each 7cm (3in) pot, which contains a mixture of 50 per cent vermiculite and 50 per cent peat. We also add a slow release, granular, high potash fertilizer (osmacote) to the peat/vermiculite mix. This toughens up the soft growth and makes it easier to overwinter the cuttings. The potash feed can also be applied to borderline hardy and slightly tender plants growing in the garden. It helps them to survive the winter and also encourages flowering.

Tim Miles, Head Gardener at The Cotswold Wildlife Park near Burford, Oxfordshire

When you buy a peony, you buy a lifetime's pleasure and, like fine wine, peonies mature with age. This planting tip from the aptly named David Root will produce lots of flowers. Do make sure that your peony isn't planted too deeply and don't worry about the old wives' tale of not disturbing them: they will move happily and settle quickly.

Peonies need good soil with lots of added organic material, a sunny position and some space round their roots, especially when the shoots emerge. When planting or moving peonies, don't plant them too deeply. The crown of the plant (where the buds are) must be 3cm (11/4in) below the soil surface, no more. If you plant the crown deeper, there'll be lots of foliage but no flowers. At the end of the year, cut back all the leaves and stems and destroy them to prevent disease. Peonies are not quick-fix plants, they take time to establish, but they live for generations.

David Root, General Manager of Kelways Ltd., Langport, Somerset

Dahlias flower their hearts out until the first frosts. They add fresh colour to the borders and they make a great cut flower for the house. The vogue is for red flowers and dark leaves, but there are fine varieties in varying shades and flower types to suit every border.

When we plant our dahlias, we make sure that the stakes to support the plants are added at the same time. We use two bamboo canes and one wooden baton measuring 2.5cm (1in) square and 90–120cm (3–4ft) high. The centre of the plant is pinched out to make the growth bushier. The dahlias are constantly cut for the house and after the first frost, they're lifted and most of the soil is removed. Then they are placed under a bench in a cold, frost-free greenhouse for the winter, before being started into growth again in early March. Our new plants are raised from cuttings and are, therefore, much easier to plant.

Graham Alcorn, Deputy Head Gardener at Mount Stuart, Isle of Bute, Scotland

Two vital parts of every gardener's propagating kit are a bag of vermiculite and a bag of (horticultural) sharp sand. Vermiculite added to compost makes a lighter, warmer mixture for seeds. Cuttings can be rooted very quickly in sharp sand and pieces of cut bulb (such as from snowdrops and narcissus) can be increased in the way described here, in the winter version of the garden shed, otherwise known as the airing cupboard.

If you want to raise more lilies, most species and cultivars can be increased by scaling during summer and autumn. First lift the bulb, or scrape away the soil around it. Break off the outer scales and dip them in fungicide or dust them with it. Place the treated scales in a plastic bag with slightly damp vermiculite or horticultural sharp sand. Seal the bag and place it in a shady spot in a warm room or the airing cupboard. In 3–5 weeks small bulbils will appear on the scales. These will develop roots and can then be potted up and grown on. They will flower within 1–2 years.

Phill Nelson of Parceval Hall Gardens near Skipton, Yorkshire

The British love their hanging baskets, but they can be one of the most time-consuming ways of adding colour to the garden. This tip, on positioning, should help with the watering. Colin Belton would also like us to be more adventurous and get away from the geranium and petunia mindset that afflicts most of us when we plan our containers and baskets.

~ Always place hanging baskets where they catch the morning sun, but avoid the midday heat. Place a small, inverted plastic bottle with the bottom removed in the centre of the arrangement, jutting 7–10cm (3–4in) above the soil. Fill it with water every day; the foliage will soon hide the bottle.

~ When choosing your plants be adventurous and draw on the wealth of tender offerings from the southern hemisphere. Spiky cordylines, rosettes of agaves and velvet-leaved plectranthus will thrive when planted with the late-flowering *Fuchsia splendens* or lobster claw (*Clianthus puniceus*). Also use dark solenostemon, streptocarpus, grasses and scented-leaved geraniums for dramatic effect.

Colin Belton, Gardens Supervisor at Logan Botanic Garden, Scotland

Heleniums, those bright, brown-centred daisies, like a high water table and they're widely grown in Holland and Germany. Paul Cook uses them at Ness, a maritime garden set close to Liverpool. Once the home of Arthur Bulley, who owned Bees Seeds, it contains a fine collection of shrubs and trees. Bulley sponsored many plant hunting expeditions, especially those undertaken by George Forrest.

Heleniums are wonderfully rich, late summer daisies, and the best way to keep them vigorous is to divide them every year. Cut them back in late September and divide them up and replant them into the same area, adding some slow-release fertilizer, such as blood, fish and bone. This will give you a good crop of flowers every year. If you're on heavy clay soil, lift your achilleas and divide and pot them up for the winter, as they often die during wet winters on heavy soil.

Paul Cook, Curator of Ness Botanic Gardens, Cheshire

The Courts Garden is one of The National Trust's best-kept secrets. The Edwardian garden has a magical, intimate quality and there are hundreds of planting ideas that every gardener can relate to and imitate. Irises are widely grown there to great effect.

Once bearded irises have flowered, don't cut the stem as it's very difficult to get a clean cut. Instead, apply pressure and push the stalk in the same direction as the rhizome, snapping it off at the base. Bearded irises also need dividing every third year – they'll reward you with much better flowers. Dig them up and sort out plump pieces of root and then cut the leaves down to a fan shape, about 10cm (4in) in height. Dig the soil over and add a light feed and then replant adding a dressing of dolomitic limestone. We always stake the irises using one green pea stick and a tie per stem as wet and windy weather can damage the blooms.

Troy Smith, Head Gardener at The Courts Garden
(The National Trust), Holt, Wiltshire

Red hot pokers – the very name inflames the passions. You either love them or you hate them. Personally, I adore them, the bigger, the brighter, the redder the better.

Kniphofias are very under used as garden plants because everyone associates them with the rampant, two-tone 'Atlanta'. However, it's possible to have pokers in flower from spring until autumn. Try some of the newer cultivars: 'Yellow Hammer', 'Timothy' (ketchup-red) and 'Jenny Bloom' (late flowering and pink). Choose a dry, sunny spot for these South African plants, nurture them well during their first two years and, when they're large enough, divide them in spring, not autumn. Take a single shoot with a root, pot up in spring and plant out the following spring. Mix them with crocosmias, golden rod and red dahlias to create a vibrant summer border.

Lester Elliott, Head Gardener at Barton Manor, Isle of Wight, where the National Collection of Kniphofia is held

Summer-flowering shrubs need pruning and the job is made more difficult by the leaves. At least in winter you can see the shape of the branches clearly before you cut. Follow this simple advice and your philadelphus will produce lots of flowers at eye level, instead of above head height.

Philadelphus, deutzias and weigelas should be summer-pruned now that they have finished flowering. They don't respond to a severe haircut. Instead, after flowering, remove one third of the old wood completely, leave a third intact and reduce the last third of the shrub by half. This encourages a succession of new shoots for next year's flowers and keeps the shape of the shrub tidy. Colchicum foliage has now died down and the bulbs can be safely lifted, divided and replanted – taking care not to damage them.

Tina Hammond, Head Gardener at The National Trust's Felbrigg Hall near Cromer, Norfolk (holder of the National Collection of Colchicum)

West Green is one of the most highly maintained gardens in Britain. Its enthusiastic manager is Marylyn Abbot, an Australian who has a 99-year lease from The National Trust.

This garden has to look stunning every time it's open, and the most challenging time of year for any gardener is the end of July. We add flower power by planting tall annuals among our old roses. Cosmos, cleome, castor-oil plant (*Ricinus*) and love-lies-bleeding (*Amaranthus*) grow up through the roses, performing until autumn. We grow these plants in pots and plant them out in late May, avoiding late frosts. The vibrant mixture of colours they provide (white, pinks, reds and violets) complements the old-rose colours perfectly. Love-in-a mist (*Nigella*) and larkspur (*Consolida*) self-seed moderately, too.

Marylyn Abbot, West Green House Garden (The National Trust) near Hook, Hampshire

Sam Youd has a money-saving tip for making that most useful thing – a cold frame. Good for cuttings, good for seeds and much more use than a greenhouse as, when properly sited, its temperature stays constant.

Make a simple cold frame by using a wooden box or an old drawer. Knock out the bottom and add a 5cm (2in) layer of compost, covered with a 2.5cm (1in) layer of horticultural sand. Take cuttings 2.5cm (1in) long of rock roses, lavenders and any silver-leaved plants. Use a sharp knife and cut on to a clean sheet of glass – both knife and glass can be sterilized with methylated spirit. Insert the cuttings into the compost, water and cover them with a sheet of white washed glass. They can be potted up individually in a month's time.
An average drawer can accommodate hundreds of cuttings.

Sam Youd, Head Gardener at Tatton Park (Cheshire County Council and The National Trust), Cheshire

At Longstock, the garden is formed by a series of interconnected ponds, fed by the River Test. Mature trees planted by John Spedan Lewis, the founder of the John Lewis Partnership, are reflected in the still waters. The waterside primulas and Himalayan blue poppies are a real feature in early summer.

We grow large numbers of primulas and meconopsis in the garden. We treat both as annuals as they are prone to dying straight after flowering. If we sow the seed straight after collection (usually late summer), it is difficult to overwinter the young plants, but if it is stored for six months it loses viability. Instead, we collect and clean the seed and place it in 35mm plastic film cases. They're put in labelled polythene bags and kept in a freezer until mid-February. This process keeps the seed young and, once taken out, it quickly germinates in trays of gritty compost inside a cold greenhouse.

Mike Stone, Head Gardener at Longstock Park Water Garden, Stockbridge Hampshire

If you summer-prune your fruit trees every year it's an easier task to identify the main leaders and the sideshoots. The pruning process produces short spurs, which in turn produce a good fruit crop.

During August we summer-prune our fruit. When you begin to prune, think carefully before you cut as you're laying down the foundations for future years. Look at each main branch and cut back each side shoot to 7cm (3in) in length. Once this is done, look at the shoots coming from those 7cm (3in) stems and shorten them back to 2.5cm (1in). This promotes fruiting buds. After pruning, feed your fruit trees with seaweed meal. This strengthens the tree, preventing pests and diseases. Winter pruning consists of shortening each main branch by one third.

Andrew Sawyer, Head Gardener at Cragside (The National Trust) near Morpeth, Northumberland

Rodney Davey is an ace propagator and he often has the job of growing rare seed for botanic gardens. He propagates a wide range of plants in a variety of ways and his skill is second to none.

You can't divide deep-rooted plants, but you can take root cuttings. Dig the whole plant up and select healthy roots, cutting pieces about 2.5cm (1in) in length. Verbascums are best done in the spring, but eryngiums and oriental poppies should be propagated during August. Put each cutting into a deep pot of sharp sand on its own, and when the plant has produced several leaves transfer it to a deep pot full of compost and then, in the following spring, plant the new plant in the garden.

Rodney Davey of R. D. Plants, Axminster, Devon

August is one of the less hectic gardening months so you'll have time to spot every gardening blunder. Plants that are in the wrong place will be looking miserable and any colour clashes will scream loudly at you. This is sound advice from the wonderfully-named Simon McPhun.

By August the magnificence of early summer is over and any planting mistakes are only too clear. When you go round and look at the garden, take a notebook and record your successes and failures. Anything that hasn't worked should be recorded and then, during the winter months, the situation can be remedied. Write down the names of all the plants that need moving, making diagrams of where they are and where they should be. Record which plants need dividing and which you need to obtain or propagate more of. Look at the mixture of colours and textures with a critical eye. If you wait until September, the moment will have passed. It's an invaluable way of improving your garden.

Simon McPhun, Head Gardener at Inverewe (The National Trust for Scotland)

Paul Picton is the authority on asters, including the Michaelmas daisies, and 40 years on the family nursery started by his father, Percy, have taught him the value of late-summer daisies of every kind. The nursery garden is a wonderful sight on a late September afternoon.

We grow a large range of late-summer and autumn-flowering perennials, and one of the real benefits is the number of butterflies we attract into our show garden. Many of the flowers are daisies and they are the perfect landing stage for butterflies. Their bold eyes are packed full of hundreds of tiny nectar-rich flowers, which help to sustain the insects. This is the time to plant New England asters (which are mildew free), echinaceas, rudbeckias, heleniums and helianthus for autumn flowering. If you have established clumps, the rule is that autumn-flowering perennials are divided in mid-spring, never in autumn.

Paul Picton, owner of The Picton Garden, Colwall near Great Malvern, Worcestershire

Most head gardeners are very short of time as many of them are responsible for several acres of garden. Anything they have found that saves valuable minutes is always worth knowing.

We've got the perfect material to put under the hedges when they're being trimmed in midsummer. Having tried plastic sheeting, which is slippery, and thick garden fleece, which is hard to handle and blows away, we've discovered that the heavy mesh used for windbreaks is ideal. It comes in a 1m (3ft) wide roll, is safe underfoot, never gets caught by the wind and is durable. Lay a length under the hedge and simply collect the clippings from the mesh. It even works with conifer cuttings on gravel and saves lots of time and mess.

Colin Roberts, Head Gardener at Auborn Hall near Lincoln

This is another good tip about cutting your conifer or yew hedges.

> Conifer and yew hedges are best cut when there's a slight dew on the leaves – it prevents any browning caused by sun scorch. These trees produce lots of resin, which can clog the shears. Stand a bucket of water, with nothing added, close by. Plunge the shears into the bucket, using a small scrubbing brush to clean the sticky resin from the blades. This ensures a clean cut and prevents damage to the branches. After cutting, top-dress the area under the hedge with bonemeal (a slow-release fertilizer) to promote root growth during winter.

Philip Whaites, Head Gardener at Wimpole Hall (The National Trust) near Royston, Cambridgeshire

Many of the hedges at Glendurgan, a garden close to the sea, are laurel – a plant loved by the Victorians, but now less popular. Yet laurel makes a fine hedge, and this method of cutting it maintains the screen but also keeps it young and green.

We use cherry laurel (*Prunus laurocerasus*) all over Glendurgan. It's kept neatly clipped in the maze, but in other areas of the garden we like it to look more natural and rounded. These informal hedges and bushes are neatened up during September, when we trim back the long shoots using a pair of secateurs. The following spring, we take a third of the stems out from the base and this encourages fresh, new growth from the heart of the laurel. Another technique we use is to trim the back half of a hedge during spring, leaving the front half intact. A year later we trim the whole hedge down to the level of the back half. Laurel makes an excellent windbreak, a rich backdrop and it's a good bee plant during April.

Steven Porter, Head Gardener at Glendurgan Garden (The National Trust) Cornwall

A wonderful gardening present is a pair of really good secateurs and a holster. With these you can dictate the limits and parameters of your plant, rather than vice versa. Martin Puddle is a third generation head gardener at Bodnant, following his father and grandfather. The magnolias there grow in a sloping valley and the view from the top is a magical sight.

Now is the time to keep an eye on your climbing plants, honeysuckles, clematis, and so on. Separate all the new, young growths before they become tangled and tie them to the wires on your wall or trellises. Prune back any dead, unhealthy or surplus shoots that you don't require. Also deadhead all summer-flowering shrubs, including roses, with freshly sharpened secateurs or a sharp knife, making a clean cut above a leaf joint. This will prevent disease and divert the plant's energy into producing more flowers and shoots, not unwanted seeds.

Martin Puddle, Head Gardener at Bodnant Garden (The National Trust), North Wales

Two National Collections – penstemons and salvias – are grown at Kingston Maurward, a formal garden surrounding a Georgian house. The house and grounds are now used as an agricultural college. Though the tender plants are mainly put out during summer, Nigel Hewish also leaves some of them outside over winter.

If you have plenty of tender plants, such as salvias, in the ground (not in pots), take a gamble and leave some in place over winter. Once they get to a certain size, many salvias and other tender plants will be able to survive. Leave the top growth on all tender plants (including penstemons) until April. The old growth protects them from the cold. Once spring arrives, don't cut them hard back. Take out all the old material, leaving any green growth intact. If you have to lift large tender plants, place them in an unheated frost-free greenhouse and then revive them in spring by repotting, feeding and watering.

Nigel Hewish, Head Gardener at Kingston Maurward Gardens, Dorset

Although most gardeners don't have access to a tractor to turn or excavate their compost heaps, they can conserve all the woody material from their garden and shred and compost it. If you can't run to a shredder, many local rubbish tips will take garden waste and turn it into compost.

We compost as much of our woody material as possible, using a brushwood chipper to make it a good size to rot down more quickly. The heaps are irrigated and turned using a small tractor and, within 12 months, make excellent compost. Local authorities often make and sell their own compost, at attractive prices, and gardeners should take advantage of these schemes. Alternatively, buying your own shredder to chop up woody material will provide you with a good source of organic material for the garden. These shreddings make excellent compost when layered with grass clippings in a conventional compost heap. Within a year they can be used for mulching and feeding.

Piers Newth, Superintendent at Harcourt Arboretum, Nuneham Courtney, Oxfordshire

109

autumn

Summer gently fades into autumn as the days shorten and although the afternoons are warm, the nights are much cooler. The resulting morning dews revive the tired garden and the sparkling quality of light found close to the autumn equinox gives the garden a jewel-box richness. While some gardeners are enjoying the grand finale, others are desperate to tidy up – to put the garden to bed. All gardeners, whether sitting back enjoying the decadent, faded glories of autumn or wielding the secateurs, will be taking stock and planning for next spring – when it all begins again.

The cow parsley family, or the umbellifers, are roguish plants that are loved by flower arrangers, and many have to be raised from seeds during late summer and autumn. Tim Ingram supplies a huge range of these and many other plants in his nursery and grows plenty in his garden; a most knowledgeable plantsman, he also grows his own nursery stock. Here he describes his recipe for success.

The best way to raise new perennial plants from seed is to collect the ripe seeds from the garden and sow them immediately. Fill individual pots with a mixture of two parts soil-based John Innes and one part vermiculite or perlite and stand the pots in water overnight. Sow the seed and cover with a fine layer of chick grit then place the pots in a cold frame or somewhere cool. Most seeds will germinate by next spring (as do astrantias and eryngiums) but some (like lilies, peonies and penstemon) will take two to three years. Saving the seed of perennials and sowing it during the following spring rarely works.

Tim Ingram of Copton Ash Gardens, Faversham, Kent

Keeping old vegetable varieties going is an important project supported by the HDRA and The National Trust. This preserves genetic inheritance, which is always useful in plant breeding. More importantly, some of the old varieties taste really good and they have amazing names.

We grow the older vegetable varieties. Although they're grown primarily for flavour, many of them are also decorative. The runner bean 'Painted Lady' has red and white flowers and is widely available. 'Lancashire Lad', is a purple-flowered pea much admired here. The strangely named haricot bean 'Hutterite Soup' is another good plant. It's the only one that doesn't need a long soak before it's used in recipes. Saving pea and bean seeds is easy. Pick the mature pods in early September, before the frosts come. Dry them off on the windowsill, store them in a cool, dry place and then sow them next year.

Alan Middling, Gardener-in-Charge at Little Moreton Hall (The National Trust) near Congleton, Cheshire

Although I've collected magnolia seeds on many an occasion, I've never managed to get them to germinate. This is not a problem experienced by Jamie Parsons, however. He sows the seeds of his rare and historically important magnolias every year with great success.

During early autumn we collect the seeds from our magnolia trees and leave the pods to ripen on a windowsill. If we left the seeds on the trees, the squirrels would eat them. The seeds are sown in early October when they're still very fresh. They have an orange coating, making them resemble orange smarties, and this has to be removed as it contains an inhibitor. You're left with large black seeds. Sow these in pots filled with 50 per cent coir and 50 per cent sand and place them outside to germinate. The pots must have a sheet of glass over them as the mice will devour every seed if given the chance. They should germinate by the following spring.

Jamie Parsons, Head Gardener at Caerhays Castle Garden near St Austell, Cornwall

It's not only Cornish mice who love to gnaw away at large seeds. Paul Champion has to net his pots of tree seeds as well. The Monkey Puzzle Avenue is one of the most famous features of Bicton College garden, which is situated close to the sea.

Here are the tricks of the trade to help you grow three of our most popular plants. The seeds of the monkey puzzle tree need to be sown when they're very fresh. Place them on their sides on the  top of moist, but not wet, compost. This prevents them from rotting. Protect the seeds from hungry mice by covering the pot with wire mesh. Acacia seeds can be also very tricky as they germinate naturally after bush fires. Pouring boiling water over the seeds emulates these conditions, spurring the seeds into growth. We also wash pittosporum seeds in a mild detergent. This removes the tarry covering that is designed to inhibit germination.

Paul Champion, Garden Manager at Bicton College, East Devon

The valley of the River Tamar, which separates Cornwall from Devon, has a balmy climate, and a hundred years ago every south-facing field grew early daffodils. Once harvested, the flowers were transported across Brunel's Tamar Bridge by the steam-driven Great Western Railway. Cotehele's Head Gardener, John Lanyon, is Cornish born and bred – and a daffodil fanatic.

Daffodils need to be planted by early September in sunny, warm positions. They look very good grown in grass, but newly planted bulbs can find it hard to push through dense turf. Lift the thinnest strip of turf possible and break it up with your fingers, then cover the bulbs, which should be planted at least 10cm (4in) below the surface. When you're planting a bulb lawn, place one large group together and then several smaller groups radiating outwards, forming an irregular, natural-looking pattern. Bulb lawns should not be mowed after November as the daffodil buds will be close to the soil surface. Once the longer days and warmer weather comes there's a rapid growth spurt and then the flowers appear.

John Lanyon, Head Gardener at Cotehele (The National Trust) near Saltash, Cornwall

When the summer bedding is past its best, those large terracotta pots can be put to good use and planted up to produce a winter container that looks good from September until May. These containers won't need watering every day either!

Take a large terracotta container – at least 23cm (9in) deep – and cover the bottom with a layer of compost 5cm (2in) deep. Lay some daffodils on the top and add another 5cm (2in) layer of compost. Then place your tulip bulbs on this. Fill the container almost to the top with compost. Now plant a small holly or conifer and surround it with winter pansies and ivy. (You could use polyanthas and vincas, too). Push some smaller bulbs (crocus and *Iris histrioides* for instance) into the top inch of compost. Deadhead as the plants and bulbs fade and you will have a pot full of colour from September until May.

Rob Fisher, Head Gardener at Elton Hall near Peterborough

Many gardeners have an empty greenhouse during the winter months. Why not use it to produce some spring colour by bringing a selection of bulbs into flower a little earlier than normal?

 Put your unheated greenhouse to good use during September and plant up some terracotta pots with varieties of *Crocus chrysanthus*: 'Cream Beauty', 'Snow Bunting' and 'Ladykiller' are all excellent. Just before they come into flower move the pots to a sheltered place in the garden, by a door or in close to a window, and enjoy some early spring colour. You can do this with other miniature bulbs and, after flowering, they can be planted out into the garden.

Paul Cook, Curator of Ness Botanic Gardens in Cheshire

The garden at Glen Chantry has an amazing array of plants and some of the most spectacular autumn performers are the colchicums, or naked ladies – so called because the flowers emerge before the leaves. Their flowers can be enhanced by growing them through ground-hugging plants.

We rely on autumn-flowering bulbs to add a touch of splendour to our garden and some of our favourite combinations use colchicums – also known as autumn crocuses. Their fresh sumptuous flowers make a wonderful contrast with the dying leaves and flowers of autumn. We grow them through perennials so the foliage supports their slender flower stems. The deep pink *Colchicum autumnale* 'Nancy Lindsay' looks lovely surrounded by a carpet of silvery foliage provided by *Artemisia stelleriana* 'Mori'. Another good combination is the low-growing magenta *Geranium* 'Anne Thomson' next to the clean white flowers of *C. speciosum* 'Album'. Brown-leaved ajugas also look good with pink colchicums.

Wol Stains of Glen Chantry, Wickham Bishops, Essex

Beth Chatto's garden is open to the public throughout the year, which makes planting spring bulbs in the autumn a difficult process. Rather than clearing the borders and guessing the whereabouts of the established clumps of bulbs, Beth Chatto adopts this system.

Beth Chatto always plants her bulbs into pots during the autumn, rather than straight into the ground. Daffodils and other bulbs are potted during September, but the tulips are potted a little later, in early November. These pots are stored outside, but care is taken not to get them too wet for the first few weeks, in case the bulbs rot off. When they are almost in flower, they are planted out into the garden. By then those bulbs already growing in the garden are visible and it's much easier to see where gaps need filling.

David Ward, Nursery Manager at the Beth Chatto Gardens near Colchester, Essex

The rock garden at Wisley has one of the best bulb lawns in the country and the dry, sandy soil is particularly suitable for cyclamen. Establishing them in your own garden is easier than you might think, especially if you follow Trevor Wiltshire's advice.

This is the time to buy autumn-flowering cyclamen. Ignore the dry tubers, which often die, instead, choose pot-grown plants with good leaves and flowers and plant them in well-drained positions. There's still time to sow cyclamen seed, although the best time is July and August, when the seed is very fresh. Use 12cm (5in) pots filled with compost, made from equal quantities of coarse limestone grit, bark, loam and leaf mould. You can also scatter the seeds of *Cyclamen coum* and *C. hederifolium* straight on to the ground. Cover the seeds with bark chippings to protect them from the birds.

Trevor Wiltshire, Superintendent of the Rock Garden at the Royal Horticultural Society Garden, Wisley, Surrey

Although daffodils need planting in early September, tulips are best planted from early November onwards. The species tulips, which flower mostly in late spring, are much smaller than their showy Dutch cousins. They are grown in an unusual way in the Victorian garden at Brodsworth Hall.

☞ Species tulips make the perfect accompaniment to our fern collection, which is planted in a sunny dell. The polystichums – a good source of green leaf in winter – need to be cut back just as the tulips come into flower, and the tulip flowers are over before the dryopteris have unfurled too widely. Species tulips should be allowed to self-seed so don't deadhead them.

☞ When planting bulbs for naturalizing, use a spade to remove the soil. Add some leafmould and some sharp sand or coarse grit and plant three to each spit. When planting any bulbs, the depth of planting should be twice the diameter of the bulb. *Tulipa tarda*, *T. praestans* and *T. humilis* are three of the easiest.

David Avery, Head Gardener at Brodsworth Hall (English Heritage) near Doncaster, Yorkshire

Lawrence Johnson created a magical garden at Hidcote on the edge of the Cotswolds. Its position on the west-facing scarp, overlooking the Vale of Evesham, ensures that every rain-bearing cloud lightens its load over it. This good advice applies to many people with gardens in wet areas.

Autumn is traditionally the time to divide herbaceous plants that have already flowered. As Hidcote lies in a high rainfall area, if we divided our plants now, we would lose many of them during winter. If you have wet, heavy soil like us, wait until spring before dividing your plants. Choose the moment when they are just starting into growth and divide them into clumps measuring about 10cm (4in) across. Take the opportunity to improve the soil before you replant your divisions by adding organic material – well-rotted – and bonemeal.

Glyn Jones, Head Gardener at Hidcote Manor Garden (The National Trust) near Chipping Campden, Gloucestershire

Those of us on the drier side of the country feel very jealous of Hidcote's rainfall. For us, September is often the best time to get stuck in and this is a money-saving tip from a thrifty head gardener in Lincolnshire.

We're all tempted to plant things when they look their best – in flower – but September is the very best time to plant all hardy perennials. Luckily for gardeners, the garden centres and nurseries often sell off their stock to lighten their workload during winter. The top growth may look shabby, but it's the roots that count. If you can go shopping now, you can buy more for your money and give the plants an excellent start. Go and search out some of those reduced plants and get them in the garden now.

Paul Gray, Head Gardener at Gunby Hall (The National Trust) near Skegness, Lincolnshire

Whenever gardeners see that annoying weed the bitter-cress, they hope and pray that the seed pods don't explode as they touch it. If only we'd known about this tip first.

Whenever you buy a garden plant from a nursery or a garden centre, it's a good idea to remove the top 2.5cm (1in) of soil from the containerized plant as this layer of soil inevitably contains seeds of bitter-cress and liverwort. Give the plant a good soak in a bucket of water, dig the hole and remove that top layer of soil, placing it at the bottom of the hole. Put the plant in the hole and cover the missing 2.5cm (1in) with a top layer of garden soil. This will stop bitter-cress and other weed seeds germinating in your garden. The layer of dry soil at ground level will also deter slugs and send the plant's roots down towards the moisture.

Nick Robinson, Head Gardener at Yalding Gardens (HDRA) near Maidstone, Kent

The borders at Great Dixter are amazingly impressive throughout spring, summer and autumn; Fergus Garrett tells us how he and Christopher Lloyd increase the flower power during the autumn.

Plants such as rudbeckias, Michaelmas daisies, chrysanthemums, perennial helianthus, sedums and *Nerine bowdenii* respond well to being moved from the open ground in full flower as long as this is done with care. These are grown in a spare plot and when an opportunity arises we give them a thorough soak with a sprinkler for at least two hours. We let them take this water in overnight so that they are absolutely turgid the next day and then dig them up with a nice rootball, taking care not to handle them too much. As each plant is planted (and this has to be done quickly after they are lifted) they are 'puddled in' ie. placed in the hole which is then filled with water and the soil then pushed in. The plant is gently firmed in using your hands making sure there is good contact between the soil and the roots. A light sprinkling of water on the leaves after planting also helps and this process ensures that the plant is under minimum stress before, during, and after moving. Keep an eye on them and make sure you plant cheek-by-jowl and get your flowers facing the same way, the aim is to make them look as if they have always grown there. This is labour-intensive but worth it!

Fergus Garrett, Head Gardener at Great Dixter, East Sussex

Victorian ladies loved ferns and their gardens always contained a fernery. Tastes changed and they fell from favour, but Martin Rickard has revived the public's interest by producing some amazing exhibits at the Chelsea Flower Show. Here's his advice.

Ferns can be planted throughout the year, but the best time to plant them is during September, October and November. As a general rule of thumb, the deciduous ferns (*Athyrium* and most *Dryopteris*) tend to like wetter conditions than the evergreen ferns (*Polystichum* and *Asplenium*). Forms of the male fern (*Dryopteris filix-mas*) and the soft shield fern (*Polystichum setiferum*) are some of the easiest to grow. Deciduous ferns are very decorative, particularly when they unfurl their crosiers in spring. When planting a fern border, grouping several ferns of the same type together does look effective but it can encourage the spread of disease. It's often safer to use a 3–4m (9–12ft) gap.

Martin Rickard of
Rickard's Hardy Ferns,
Tenbury Wells,
Worcestershire

Bob Brown is known as one of the most entertainingly funny gardeners, as well as one of the most knowledgeable nurserymen.

If you have heavy clay soil like we do at the nursery, never plant any herbaceous perennials after 1 September: you're almost bound to lose them. Remember the 'Three Wise Men' and start planting again on Epiphany – 6 January – and do the bulk of your planting in spring.

Bob Brown of Cotswold Garden Flowers in Badsey, near Evesham, Worcestershire

The two gardeners at The Old Vicarage in East Ruston, Norfolk are known for their flair and artistry in the garden and this winning combination is one of their autumn favourites.

One of our favourite plant combinations uses hydrangeas and hardy fuchsias. Hydrangeas fade with great dignity and, though they may have been brash in July, by September the large flowerheads are wonderfully muted pale greens flecked with touches of pink and red. Two of our favourite mopheads are *Hydrangea macrophylla* 'Madame Emile Moullière', which turns lime-green as it fades, and *H. macrophylla* 'Ayesha', which fades to a pale lilac. These versatile, easily propagated plants, tolerate semi-shade or full shade and thrive in woodland. They deserve a place in every garden and, mixed with hardy fuchsias, will provide colour over many months.

Alan Gray, co-owner of the Old Vicarage at East Ruston, Norfolk

Rodmarton Manor, a romantic sleeping beauty of a house, was designed by the Barnsley brothers, key members of the Arts and Crafts Movement. The yew-hedged double borders, which surround a long path leading down to the stone summer house, are beautifully planted by the owner Simon Biddulph.

We have four long herbaceous borders and we have a regular order of overhauling one every year. This seems a daunting task, but we make a start in September when the weather is pleasant and the soil is dry. By doing it then, we can see precisely which plant is which – some are still flowering. We cut down each group of plants, dig them up, discard any bits we don't want and replant those we intend to keep. We don't disturb peonies, but most other plants are lifted and then put back. They have plenty of time to settle down again before the winter.

Simon Biddulph, owner of Rodmarton Manor, midway between Tetbury and Cirencester, Gloucestershire

As fallen leaves rot down they produce toxins and harbour slugs, so gathering them up is advisable. A still autumn day makes this task an easier proposition.

Collect up your leaves as soon as they fall, but before they get wet. This will prevent them from becoming a wet, soggy mess and damaging the lawn. Place the dry leaves in black plastic bin-liners, tie these up and leave them somewhere shady and dry for 12 months. Then use the resulting well-rotted leaf-mould for mulching and for digging into the soil. If you do this every year, you will have a supply of rich compost every autumn.

Matthew Wilson, Curator of the Royal Horticultural Society Garden, Hyde Hall, Essex

In some areas of the garden cutting down and tidying has to be done now, and different gardeners have their own way of disposing of the debris. The end result is still the same – lots of rich organic material to add fertility.

This is the perfect time to make a compost heap. As you clear the borders, cut each stem into 15cm (6in) lengths and place them in a wheelbarrow. Smaller pieces rot down more quickly and the cutting process helps to mix the different thicknesses of stem. Put them on the heap and add a layer of grass clippings and some water if the stems are very dry. Once complete, cover the heap with a wooden board or an old piece of carpet and it leave for 12 months. The resulting compost should be like a good cake – not too dry and not too wet – and the crumbly mixture will add valuable humus to the soil. Use it to top-dress the borders with a 5cm (2in) layer, preferably in spring.

Linda Roberts, Gardener-in-Charge at Snowshill Manor (The National Trust) near Broadway, Gloucestershire

Mike Scott has the ultimate leaf gathering tool and it's one that few of us have in the shed. He also uses something many of us do have in an unusual way.

The best garden tool ever invented is the rubber rake, which collects the leaves from borders quickly and without damaging the plants. It's light and comes in two widths. Many gardeners have never seen these rakes and use the metal-tined variety instead, but these cannot be dragged over a border without tearing the leaves, while a rubber rake glides over the plants effortlessly. The best way to collect leaves on the lawn is to use a rotary mower. It chops them up and pulls them into the grass box. The mixture of leaf and grass rots down very quickly when added to the compost heap.

Mike Scott, Head Gardener at Hare Hill (The National Trust), Prestbury in Cheshire

Some gardeners don't need a rubber rake – just a large spade and a good technique!

We garden on heavy clay and start digging early, before the worst of winter sets in. One of our garden volunteers, a retired nurseryman, is known as 'dig-it-in-Jim' because he doesn't pull out any of the old annuals when he digs. He has developed a technique of chopping the plant material up as he goes, even 2m (6ft) sunflowers get the 'dig-it-in-Jim' treatment. It saves a journey to the compost heap and back again. We've all learnt the technique and it does get the nutrients straight back into the soil – so dig-it-in like Jim.

David Standing, Garden Manager at Gilbert White's Garden, Selborne, Hampshire

The garden at Hadspen is one of the most admired in the country and this green tip from Sandra and Nori Pope is eminently practical.

⌘ We cut down the perennials in September, but leave the debris in neat piles in the borders. These heaps provide shelter for the ladybirds, lacewings and other insects during the winter. When the insects emerge during the following spring, they're ready to help you keep the garden free of pests – we don't have an aphid problem here. Lots of toads shelter in the debris, too, and they eat the slugs. We collect the debris up during February; by then it has rotted down, so there isn't as much to collect.

Nori and Sandra Pope who garden at Hadspen House, Somerset

The autumn tidy up is a very thorough one at Ivy Cottage, but it's a good tip to be aware that the hollow stems of some plants can hold the water. Winters are also getting warmer and wetter, and this means that weeds are more of a problem, and for longer.

I garden on greensand, which holds the moisture and provides lots of lush growth. Now that we're getting warmer, wetter winters, we have to be more careful than ever to tidy up during autumn. I remove all decaying foliage close to the ground as snails and slugs hide away in this debris during the winter. The perennial plants are cut down as low as possible, especially those with hollow stems – delphiniums and lupins for instance. If not removed these hollow stems fill with water and cause rot, possibly destroying the whole plant. Keep the garden well weeded, too, as warmer winters allow seeds to carry on growing.

Anne Stevens, owner of Ivy Cottage near Dorchester, Dorset

Bamboo is widely grown at Trebah, a Cornish garden that enjoys a warm, maritime climate in which winter wet (and not cold) is the enemy.

This is the time to thin out your clumps of bamboo by removing all the old dead culms before the new shoots emerge next spring. Leave any fresh newer growth intact for next year, but take out any ragged stems. It's also time to protect your tree ferns. Cut pieces of envirofleece 60cm (24in) square and place several of these in the crowns of the tree ferns to protect next year's crop of fronds. Fleece should also be wrapped around other tender plants, but do take cuttings as well.

Darren Dickey, Head Gardener at Trebah Gardens near Falmouth, Cornwall

Philip Astley has another very good use for garden fleece.

The last half of September is the best time of year to sow grass as the newly germinated seed has time to establish good roots before winter sets in. Deep dig the area and add some fertile loam and some coarse sand or grit. Use an autumn lawn fertilizer, then sow and water the seed in well. Cover the whole area with horticultural fleece. This will keep the birds away, keep the moisture in and trap the heat, creating ideal conditions for germination. Remove the fleece after a month, by then the grass will be well established and able to withstand wintry weather.

Philip Astley, Head Gardener of Cottesbrooke Hall, Northampton

Cabbage White butterflies are the bane of every gardener's life, but there is a solution that doesn't involve chasing them round with a net.

We garden organically here and this year our cabbages have been under attack from Cabbage White butterflies throughout the summer. If you have problems, use a physical solution, rather than a chemical one, and cover your plants with fine mesh (one with 1mm holes). This will keep the butterflies away from your plants but allows the rain to penetrate and the air to circulate, keeping your plants healthy. We don't use netting in our ornamental vegetable garden and the most helpful insect is the much maligned wasp, which eats the small, young caterpillars.

Mark Jeffery, Head Gardener at Culross Palace (The National Trust for Scotland), Dunfermline, Fife

If you're very lucky the birds will eat your slugs and snails for you. Patricia Cooper sets out to attract them with a gourmet diet of seeds in her Norfolk garden.

Attracting birds into the garden is a priority here so we leave many of our seed heads intact. We've found that the seed-eating finches have their own preferences. The siskins go for blue chicory, *Carex pendula* and *Oenothera stricta* 'Sulphurea'. The greenfinches strip all the seeds from the biennial milk thistle (*Silybum marianum*) and the goldfinches prefer the tall, silvery thistle (*Onopordum acanthium*). Bullfinches strip *Geranium phaeum* and the native herb-Robert in the wild garden. The goldfinches enjoy the verbascum seeds and the biennial evening primrose. Growing some of these will lure these handsome birds into your garden, too.

Patricia Cooper, owner of Magpies, Mundford near Downham Market, Norfolk

The West Country is famous for its cider, but the slugs still prefer the beer.

We've never had a vast slug problem here as we have plenty of thrushes and blackbirds in the garden – and no cats. We stopped using bait a couple of years ago and went over to the large, square slug 'pubs'. We fill these with the cheapest bitter we can find and then empty them once a week. Usually we catch 20 or more slugs and small snails in each. Gardeners tend to be very vigilant early in the year, but slugs can damage the shoots of delphiniums and campanulas during the autumn. Using slug traps in September will help protect these and other susceptible plants.

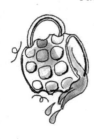

Floyd Summerhayes of Tintinhull House Garden (The National Trust) near Yeovil, Somerset

Keeping the fertility and the warmth in the top layers of soil is always a problem when winter sets in; Lizzie Gilbert of Sudeley Castle adopts an organic method.

We keep the fertility in the upper layers of the soil in the Heritage Vegetable Garden by planting a green manure crop in late autumn. The easiest plant is *Phacelia tanacetifolia* – it's very easy to dig in. The seeds are broadcast sown, watered if the soil is dry and then left to grow. Shortly before we're ready to replant, we dig the crop in (before it's flowered), leave it for two weeks and then plant. The green manure crop makes the soil more fertile and the decomposition process warms the soil. Once our seeds are planted, they get away quickly.

Lizzie Gilbert, Garden Manager of Sudeley Castle Gardens, Winchcombe, Gloucestershire

This award-winning garden, open under The National Gardens Scheme, is an inspiration for owners of small gardens. The modern design, the fun factor, the unusual plants, the good ideas and the overall visual effect have made this garden runner-up in both the BBC Gardener of the Year and *The Daily Mail*'s Garden of the Year competitions. Like many others, I think it deserved to win.

The conventional wisdom on over-wintering banana plants is to wrap them thoroughly by making a structure with wire and packing it with straw. This covers the crown of the plant completely and we've found that it makes them prone to rotting off in the warm, wet winters we get in the south. Instead, at the end of October or early November, we move the potted plant into a sheltered place against the house. We use the old leaves – folding them up around the plant as protection – but leave the stem uncovered. To produce the massive leaves that make such a statement in the garden, bananas need to be grown in a substantial, roomy pot and fed and watered well – we apply seaweed extract and soluble plant food every two weeks.

Ralph Cade, co-owner of 8 Grafton Park Road, Worcester Park, London

Exotic plants are gaining in popularity and this wise advice should prevent gardeners from losing their tender charges in British winters.

The sun still has some warmth in it during the second half of October and this is the last opportunity to dry off containers of half-hardy yuccas, cycads, agaves and bromeliads. On a sunny day, bring them into an unheated greenhouse and open the doors and windows. Let the heat of the sun dry out the compost and the rosette before the cold, dank weather sets in. Keep the greenhouse windows and doors open whenever possible during the winter. By late February, the sun will be strong enough to warm the greenhouse, and watering can start once again. Always water in the morning, making sure all the doors and windows are fully open and then the excess water can evaporate in the sun. A sunny porch can also be used.

Nicholas Wray, Superintendent of the University of Bristol Botanic Garden

Historically, the three great gardens of the Cotswolds were Hidcote Manor, Kiftsgate and Abbotswood. Abbotswood is now privately owned, but opens for The National Gardens Scheme and The Red Cross. The house, once the home of Mark Fenwick, has a stone gable of immense proportions and there are some other fine Lutyen's features, including a round pond.

We grow many hybrid teas and floribundas and we don't wait until spring to prune them – we take them back hard during late autumn. We clean up all the debris and burn it to prevent the spread of disease and then mix a tar-based garden disinfectant, which also contains a fungicide (Armillatox) then, using a watering can fitted with a rose, drench each rose and the surrounding soil. We use about one can for each and then we fork through the soil around each rose, too. Finally, we add another drench to the soil. This also prevents the spread of disease. The roses are heavily mulched with manure during March.

Martin Fox, Head Gardener at Abbotswood near Stow-on-the-Wold, Gloucestershire

Rupert Ely inherited his knowledge and enthusiasm for trees and shrubs from his grandfather who taught him the names in his garden. Now his nursery sells a wide range of these fine trees, shrubs and herbaceous plants. A trip there always involves a hazardous journey back for me – the car is always so full of plants, I have to peep through branches to see the road, fore and aft. More importantly, you get good advice about what and what not to grow. My advice is, don't take any passengers!

When you plant a new tree, buy a mulch mat as well. These keep the weeds down and conserve moisture. Trees that have had a mulch mat put in place when planted grow much more vigorously – after ten years they're twice as large as those planted in grass. You can mulch a newly planted tree with garden compost or well-rotted manure. If you do, spread it loosely around the tree, not tightly packed against the trunk.

Rupert Ely of The Place for Plants, East Bergholt Place, Suffolk

Ken Potts is equally knowledgeable. He used to work at the Bedgebury National Pinetum and chose his current home because of the acid soil. This allows him to grow a huge range of choice trees and shrubs; the rest of garden, close to the house, is mainly herbaceous.

Gardeners who prefer to enjoy their fireworks before 5 November have plenty of shrubs to chose from, particularly if they have acid soil. The following shrubs will all erupt into fiery displays for several weeks: *Disanthus cercidifolius*, fothergilla, stewartias, liquidambar and varieties of *Acer palmatum*. Gardeners with alkaline soils should grow *Hydrangea quercifolia*, *Prunus sargentii*, *Euonymus alatus* and the cotoneasters *C. horizontalis* and *C.* 'John Waterer' to get the same effect. Add lots of bulky humus to alkaline soils to encourage more colour and try some of the borderline plants like witch-hazel (*Hamamelis*), which also colour up well.

Ken Potts, owner of Chiff Chaffs, Bourton, Dorset

Barbara Joseph of The Dingle Nursery and Garden is another expert on trees and shrubs. The autumn colour there is spectacular, too, and she offers this excellent advice.

A year of high rainfall will produce lots of lush growth on trees and shrubs. This will make them more vulnerable than usual to damage during the autumn and winter. Act now, shorten back any lush, soft growth on all hardy trees and shrubs before the storms set in. Also, check that your trees are adequately staked to prevent wind rock. The main pruning will still need doing late next spring, but shortening back the soft growth now will preserve your shrubs and trees through the winter.

Barbara Joseph of The Dingle Nursery and Garden near Welshpool, Powys

Once the leaves turn and fall it's possible to propagate some new shrubs – this is how to do it.

The moment when the leaves have dropped is the perfect time to take hardwood cuttings from deciduous shrubs. Choose sturdy shoots produced this year, making sure there are no blemishes or diseases. The cuttings should be pencil thickness and about 25cm (10in) long. Cut just beneath the node at the bottom end of the cutting and just above the bud at the upper end. These cuttings can be placed in the open ground, but you must plant them deeply, burying about three quarters of each cutting.
In heavy soil, line the trench with sand or grit to prevent waterlogging. Leave the cuttings *in situ* until the following autumn, then plant them out.

Bob Mitchell, Honorary Curator of St Andrews Botanic Garden, The Canongate, St Andrews, Fife

Those autumn leaves can be quickly made into compost, following this recipe.

By the end of September we are beginning to accumulate lots of autumn leaves. These are mixed with grass clippings and well-rotted horse or cow manure. The mixture is left until February or early March and, when partially rotted down, is shredded to make a fine and nutritious mulch, which feeds the plants, conserves moisture and prevents weed seeds from germinating. This is a good way of using autumn leaves to produce a nourishing mulch within months. Shredding accelerates the decomposition process allowing the worms to get really busy.

Charles Wade, Head Gardener of Holker Hall near Grange-over-Sands, Cumbria

For those of us with full compost heaps, this is the perfect way to keep warm during an autumn afternoon.

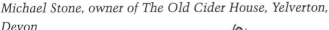 We maintain several compost heaps and now is the time to empty one or two of them and spread them on to the kitchen garden. In order to prevent the goodness leaching out and the benefit being lost, we cover the ground with black agricultural polythene, which is cheap and comes in huge rolls. When we take this off in the spring, the ground is that little bit warmer, and the compost is ready just to be turned in as a humus-rich mulch. This activity makes some much needed space in the compost bins for the herbaceous material we are cutting down at the end of the year. The newly filled bins will be ready to empty next autumn.

Michael Stone, owner of The Old Cider House, *Yelverton, Devon*

Errdig has one of The National Trust's best kept orchards. Storing the apples is one of the late-season jobs. Done properly, many British apple varieties will keep until spring.

☞ When storing apples, choose a cool airy outhouse or garage and wrap each apple in newspaper to stop maggots and mould spreading through the store. Varieties such as 'Sturmer Pippin', 'Ashmead's Kernel' and 'Joaneten' (a corruption of 'June eating') keep for many months. Another method for storing apples for just a few weeks is to place 2.25–4.5kg (5–10lbs) of unblemished fruit in a large plastic bag that has 5–10 holes in it.

☞ If your trees suffer from apple canker, which produces swollen lesions on branches and trunks, spray them with a copper fungicide just before leaf fall.

Glyn Smith of Errdig (The National Trust) near Wrexham

Few of us realize that apples have an ancient heritage and that Roman soldiers knew how to graft and grow apples. Generations of plant breeding have produced hundreds of varieties and we should find out more about which ones evolved in our part of the country.

Every area has its own varieties of apple. They're the ones that grow really well on the local soil and in the local climate and often thrive in only one or two counties. However, now that they are becoming more readily available from specialist nurseries, it's often possible to find them. Head for a local 'Apple Day' and research which ones grow well close to your home. In Cumbria we do well with 'Square Lemon', 'Keswick Codling' and 'Scotch Bridget'. Choose dwarf or semi-dwarf apple trees and plant them in an open position, in grass if possible.

Chris Braithwaite, Gardener-in-Charge at Acorn Bank Garden (The National Trust), Cumbria

Hardy fuchsias can go on late into the year if they escape the frosts. In the warm coastal areas close to Combe Martin they flower all year long. Most of us aren't so lucky.

☞ When your hardy fuchsias have finished flowering, lightly trim the growth to prevent the wind from rocking the plants. Next year, in late spring, cut them hard back. By then the sap will be rising and they will quickly grow away. May and June are the best planting months. Choose a mature second year plant with a woody base. 'Margaret', 'Edith' and 'Mrs Popple' are excellent hardy fuchsias and perfect companions for spring bulbs. The ideal garden position is a well-drained site in semi-shade. If drainage is poor, dig a deep hole, 60cm (2ft) wide, half fill it with rubble then plant the fuchsia on top.

Roger Gilbert of Silver Dale Fuchsias, Combe Martin, North Devon

The last mow of the year is the moment gardeners usually long for – then we can put our feet up, or can we?

After the last mow of the year we spike our lawns to improve the drainage, which discourages moss. We also gather up the last of the leaves lying on the lawns as, in the early stages of decomposition, they produce toxic substances that cause the grass to die back. We tidy up carefully, but not ruthlessly, in the borders, leaving the stems of herbaceous plants at a height of 22cm (9in) or more. These make useful markers next spring. Hydrangea heads are left intact as ladybirds shelter in the leaf axils and we try not to disturb hedgehogs, which often overwinter in leaves in the borders.

Robin Allan, Head Gardener at Hardwick Hall (The National Trust) near Chesterfield, Derbyshire

David Austin's English roses are world-famous and the display garden on the nursery has to be meticulously maintained. These expert tips from the head gardener will make your roses produce more flowers.

Tie in the long stems of rambling roses now, before the winter gales break them off. Only shorten the stems if really necessary as it is these that produce next year's roses. We wind them around wire supports, but they can be loosely wound around poles or other frameworks. Never tie them tightly and never use plastic ties as the rose will die back to these. Instead, lightly fix with string, raffia or garden wire.

November is the best month for planting bare-root roses. Dig holes down to 60cm (24in) and incorporate lots of manure or garden compost into the soil making a small heap above ground level – it will soon level out.

Richard Stubbs, Head Gardener at David Austin Roses Show Garden, Bowling Green Lane, Albrighton, Wolverhampton

Dahlias are another frost-tender autumn glory. They're grown in profusion at Leeds Castle and the tubers are carefully kept from year to year.

When the frost blackens your dahlias cut the tops back to 10–15cm (4–6in). Lay the stems over the plants for about a week; this encourages the tubers in the ground to ripen and harden. Then, on a fine day, lift them carefully and turn them upside down for a few hours, which allows any moisture to drain from the hollow stems and the crown. Leaving a little soil round the tubers – it prevents them from becoming too dry – store them in a frost-free place where it's cool and airy. Check them once a month and discard any that show signs of mould.

Derek Horton, Garden Manager at Leeds Castle near Maidstone, Kent

Gardeners may be driven indoors during the worst of the wintry weather but even then they use their time to plan next year's campaign. They browse through seed catalogues, read all the articles they didn't get time to look at earlier in the year and thoroughly enjoy the long winter evenings of inactivity, hopefully by a log fire. Outside, the garden is stripped bare and it's possible to assess it and redesign it where necessary. Now is the time to undertake long-term landscape work, whenever the weather allows. Though much of the time it is dark and gloomy, there are those magical days when frost or snow bring a sparkle to the garden. As the days go by, there are glimmers of hope, an unfurling catkin or a sleepy bumble bee, that reassure us that spring is surely coming.

No relaxing, we're still in training for next year according to Mike Thurlow, who's getting ready for some heavy gardening work.

Take a good look at your hand tools and replace any damaged ones – it's easier to break them in during the winter months. Sharpen the blades of all secateurs and spades, then soak a cloth with linseed oil and, having stripped back the handles to the bare wood, apply a liberal coat. The linseed provides a soft surface preventing blisters and chafing. Never put your tools away when they're damp or muddy, always scrape the mud away with a piece of slate, and hang a rag dipped in linseed oil next to the tools to remind you to wipe handles and blades after every use. Get the mower serviced straight after the last cut, ready for action next spring.

Mike Thurlow, Head Gardener at the Audley End (English Heritage and HDRA) organic kitchen garden, Saffron Walden, Essex

The bird life at Beatrix Potter's garden, Hill Top, won't have to worry about their food supply as this garden is full of seed heads. The cold winter mornings transform the spent flower borders into a magical affairs, the hoar-frost decorating umbels of fennel, the solid cones of the rudbeckia and the ramrod-straight stems of the aster.

At Hill Top I like to leave herbaceous perennials until they have produced their seeds before cutting them back at the end of the year. The seeds provide a valuable food source for birds, such as goldfinches and sparrows, which need all the help they can get before winter sets in. The bonus for the gardener is that after a frost or heavy dew, the garden takes on a whole new beauty. Leaving a log or brush pile in a corner of the garden to gently decay, will create an ideal habitat for insects and other wildlife, including toads.

Peter Tasker, Head Gardener at Hill Top (The National Trust) near Ambleside, Cumbria

While the toads are hibernating at Hill Top in Cumbria, down in Kent it's all action.

Don't sit by the fire during November and December, make the most of the daylight hours. Whenever the weather allows, get outside and work: it will pay dividends next spring. Lift, divide and replant all herbaceous perennials if needed, except for kniphofias and grasses. Prune back roses and shrubs, tidy up all debris thoroughly and remove all seeding weeds as you dig the borders. Although you'll get another bite of the cherry in March, by then there are many other demands. When spring arrives, your borders will only need lightly forking over, allowing you to get on elsewhere.

Sarah Cook, Head Gardener at Sissinghurst Castle Garden (The National Trust) near Cranbrook, Kent

On the Welsh coast, some serious groundwork is going on to prepare for next summer's highlight – the sweet pea tunnel. There's no shortage of well-rotted manure down on the farm.

We grow sweet peas all along both sides of our pergola, which stretches for nearly 28m (90ft). They start to flower in June and constant picking and deadheading keeps them going throughout the summer and on until autumn. The secret of growing them well lies in preparing a deep trench and filling it with organic material, which we do during the winter. We use well-rotted farm manure, but you can use garden compost mixed with damp newspapers. The young plants are tied to supports and soon put down deep roots.

Dilwyn Vaughan, owner of Penlan-Uchaf Farm Gardens, Fishguard, Pembrokeshire

For those of you who are driven indoors, the perfect plant for the short days is the easiest-to-grow orchid, the cymbidium. You have to be cruel to be kind.

Many gardeners are far too kind to their cymbidiums and they sit in the corner of a room, producing lots of leaves and no flowers. Cymbidiums are best summered outdoors in dappled shade and left outside until the nights begin to get cool. They mustn't get frosted, but they do need to experience cool night-time temperatures of around 7°C (45°F) and warmer days. This mimics the conditions in their native Himalayas and initiates flowering. Bring them indoors during October and find them a cool – not too centrally heated, north-facing position and they will produce lots of flowers.

Christopher Bailes, Curator of the Royal Horticultural Society Garden, Rosemoor, Devon

If an orchid is a little too exotic, try growing a peace lily instead.

One of the easiest plants to grow during the dark days of winter is the peace lily (*Spathiphyllum*). These plants, though they look tropical, tolerate low light levels and do not need a great deal of heat; up to 16°C (61°F) is fine. Give them a weekly dose of houseplant food and keep them moist, but not water-logged, and they will flower throughout the winter. After flowering, cut off each stem. Repot during late spring and they should flower again next winter.

Karl Hansen, Director of The Living Rainforest near Newbury, Berkshire

... or a streptocarpus.

Streptocarpus flower for longer than any other house plant – from spring until late autumn – and they're tough, easy plants. They thrive in temperatures that don't fall below 10°C (50°F). They need good strong light, but not direct sunlight – east or west windows are best. The secret lies in not overwatering – streptocarpus don't like standing in water – keep the compost moist and only water when the surface feels dry to the touch. Feed them with a high-potash feed (tomato feed will do) every two weeks when they are in flower. They can be repotted in a peat-based compost between November and March and leaf cuttings can be taken from March onwards.

Gareth Dibley of Dibleys Nurseries, Ruthin, North Wales

Or put the greenhouse to good use and overwinter some auriculas for a spring display.

Try to buy auriculas when they're in flower – during spring. Purchase established pot-grown plants, not plug plants. A healthy auricula should make lots of fine roots and, if in doubt when you're buying, carefully up-end the pot and examine the roots. We repot our auriculas in November: the secret is to give them an airy, friable compost made from 50 per cent peat, 25 per cent grit and 25 per cent loam. Put them in a cold greenhouse during winter, keeping them on the dry side. When spring comes aim to keep the compost slightly moist. Auriculas make excellent specimens for an outdoor plant theatre.

Joe Shardlow of Martin Nest Nurseries near Gainsborough, Lincolnshire

Rhubarb is a Yorkshire delicacy and it's forced in darkened sheds where the only noise is the pop of the sheaths springing from the emerging buds. The freshly stewed rhubarb can be eaten with custard or the juice added to champagne or vodka. When the crowns are dormant, the gardeners at Harlow Carr get busy. They divide and replant the 30 species and 115 different cultivars that make up their National Collection.

November and December is the perfect time to divide your established rhubarb plants, so long as the ground isn't frozen. Lift the mature crowns and keep the young pieces, discarding any old pieces of root. Dig a large hole, fill it with manure and replant the new crowns, spacing them well. Add a top-dressing of nitrogen-based fertilizer. You should divide rhubarb crowns every fourth year and, remember, don't harvest the stalks after July as they're very acidic. Always pull the rhubarb away from the crown, don't cut it.

Andrew Hart, Curator of the Royal Horticultural Society Garden, Harlow Carr near Harrogate, Yorkshire

This piece of advice is one of the best I know for novice gardeners. I'd also add that a gentle stroll around the neighbourhood after Sunday lunch will reveal what other gardeners are growing successfully. That way you can avoid expensive mistakes, such as trying to grow an acid-loving rhododendron when your soil is chalky.

A good way to restock a garden with plants is to visit your local garden centre or nursery once a month and only buy plants that are in flower. If you do this for a year, not only will you spread the cost of buying all those plants, you'll also have something in bloom every month of the year.

Peter Tasker, Head Gardener at Hill Top (The National Trust) near Ambleside, Cumbria

I have found this tip invaluable.

When someone asks you to name a plant in your garden, there's nothing more frustrating than grovelling on the ground, only to bring up a faded label that can't be read. When you plant your treasure, put the label in a pot and write the date of planting and where it is on the back in pencil. This will help you enormously in the years to come!

Bob Brown of Cotswold Garden Flowers in Badsey, near Evesham, Worcestershire

One of the nagging anxieties at the back of every gardeners' mind is whether the mower will start after its long winter rest. The garden team at Coleton Fishacre have been there, done it and got the t-shirt. They can relax.

Drain down any pieces of machinery that are run on unleaded petrol or a two-stroke mixture. Both substances go off within weeks and it's unlikely that your mower, hedge cutter, and so on, will start next spring as the fuel will have deteriorated. Either drain them using the tap or by tipping them upside down, or run them out of fuel. Check the spark plugs and blades and get all mowers serviced before spring starts.

Andrew McCoryn and the team at Coleton Fishacre Garden (The National Trust) near Dartmouth, Devon

Being a Yorkshire girl I understand this thrifty tip completely. Look after your garden tools and they will last you a life time. I expect the spades are really short in many a Yorkshireman (and woman's) garden.

I've never known a gardener wear out a good garden spade – the blades don't break, they just get shorter. Ours are made of the finest Sheffield steel and after every single use we clean them thoroughly. This only takes a few seconds and a clean sharp spade makes the job easier. We have a bucket of sand, with a layer of oil on the surface, just by the door. As we come in at the end of the day, we plunge the blade into the bucket of sand and pull it out again. Then we wipe the blade over with an oily rag and thoroughly dry the handle. My own spade has lasted me 25 years and will go on until I retire. The blade gleams like the surface of a mirror. The back end of the year is the perfect time to have a look at your garden tools.

Brian Deighton, Head Gardener
at Castle Howard, Yorkshire

Looking after your garden seats is just as important; this mixture is the best thing for all your wooden furniture.

As winter sets in, extend the life of your garden furniture by bringing it inside. Allow it to dry off for several weeks and lightly sand it. Then apply a mixture made from equal parts of turpentine and raw linseed oil. Check that the linseed oil is raw and not cooked. Apply at least two good coats. If you can't take your furniture inside, cover it with a tarpaulin or similar sheet and then treat it as the weather allows.

Andrew McCoryn and the team at Coleton Fishacre Garden (The National Trust) near Dartmouth, Devon

Part of the gardeners' art is beating the birds, whether it be to the strawberries, apples or …

Cut your holly sprigs for Christmas in early December before the birds strip the berries. Hang them up high in a cool garage or a shed as the mice will steal the berries if they are laid on the ground. The sprigs keep for weeks. Most hollies are males or females and need a partner to produce berries, but *Ilex aquifolium* 'J.C. van Tol' is a self-fertile holly that berries reliably on its own. Others that berry heavily, with the help of a male bush, are *I. aquifolium* 'Alaska' (a purple-stemmed, green-leaved, red-berried female) and 'Bacciflava' (an orange-berried female).

David Beardall, Head Gardener at York Gate (Gardeners' Royal Benevolent Society) Adel, near Leeds

If it isn't the birds, it's the mice you have to watch!

Remove the leaves from your hellebores soon after Christmas. This prevents the mice from eating the flower buds. If the leaves are left on, the mice shelter under them and nibble the buds, destroying all the flowers. Removing the leaves now also prevents hellebores from getting black spot disease. After cutting off the leaves, feed the plants with well-rotted manure or garden compost as they are greedy feeders and will produce many more flowers if well fed. If you need to divide them, wait until after August as by then the buds have formed. Use two forks and split them into quarters and then replant.

Lesley Rootham, Head Gardener at The Old Rectory, Burghfield, Berkshire

Every gardener needs an excuse to escape to the greenhouse. It's a retreat – the modern equivalent of the sulking room or the boudoir.

The first weeks of the new year are a good time to plant seeds of alpines, trees and shrubs, such as acer, sambucus, sorbus and holly. All these need a spell of cold weather to germinate – called stratification. Use round pots filled with gritty compost, and once sown, liberally cover each pot with grit to prevent the formation of algae. Place in a cold frame and keep the pot moist during summer to prevent drying out. Germination varies, sometimes taking up to a year or even longer.

Debbie Rees, Garden Manager at The Van Kampen Gardens, Hampton Court, near Leominster, Herefordshire

Well kept paths, hedges and lawns are vital in gardens that open to the public; work starts early at Cranborne Manor Garden.

- January is the best month to deal with weeds on gravel paths. Use a pre-emergent and post-emergent weedkiller specially designed for paths. Rake the gravel thoroughly and mix the solution well – the granules must be totally dissolved. Water or spray the mixture on the paths, following directions. This treatment, applied now, will prevent weeds germinating for the whole year.

- Many gardeners have an unheated greenhouse that is empty (or partly empty) for the winter months. Sow a crop of mixed salad leaves now for an early crop.

Les Dinan, Head Gardener at Cranborne Manor Garden, Wimborne Minster, Dorset

This garden is one of the little-known gems of North-umberland, a hop, skip and a jump away from Wallington (The National Trust) and close to Belsay Castle (English Heritage) as well.

Our intensively gardened acre was made on a soil-less garden and we used a 7cm (3in) layer of river sand over paths and the flower beds. This dense layer stopped the weed seeds from germinating and any subsequent weeds were easily pulled up. We chose a pink-tinged sand, which contrasts well with green leaves and gives the garden a touch of fantasy. Many of our annual, biennial and perennial plants self-seed generously into it. Worms eventually pull the sand down into the soil – creating better drainage – and after three years the layer needs replenishing. The sand doesn't alter the pH of the soil or tread into the house, but choose the colour carefully.

Frank Lawley, Herterton House (garden and nursery) near Morpeth, Northumberland

One of these tips involves half mooning. It isn't what you may imagine though! Seriously, the wealth of expertise among trained gardeners who started life in the bothy and worked their way up never ceases to amaze me. These two tips sound obvious, but they are both gems.

- My father taught me that when half mooning (edging a bed) it is best to angle the tool slightly outwards rather than straight down. This exaggerates the edge, making it look deeper, and it aids drainage, which in turn stops the weed problem caused when damp soil and seeds congregate in the bottom of the groove at the lawn edge.

- The correct way to use a pair of garden hand-shears is to hold one blade still and move the other blade, taking the cutting blade to the stationary one. It takes some learning but the results are much more accurate. This is something every novice gardener was taught as a young lad.

Robert Vernon of the Bluebell Nursery and Arboretum near Ashby-de-la-Zouch, Leicestershire

Owners of small gardens don't have the opportunity to grow many trees. This tip, also from Robert Vernon, is for a wooded area devoted entirely to trees, not a mixed border.

 During November and December clear the areas around the base of the trees and apply granular weedkiller (Kerb Granules) to keep the area close to the tree weed-free. This treatment lasts for 12 months. It cannot be used close to non-woody material, but in wooded areas it is invaluable. Remember never to strim close to the base of a tree as it will damage the trunk.

Robert Vernon of the Bluebell Nursery and Arboretum near Ashby-de-la-Zouch, Leicestershire

Nowadays when garden centres sell containerized plants almost exclusively, it's easy to forget that specialist growers also sell bare-rooted trees. The team at Coleton Fishacre recommend them.

We advocate the buying of bare-root trees, which we find grow away far more successfully than containerized ones. They will be delivered from November onwards. When they arrive, it's crucial to keep the roots covered and store them in a frost-free place. Then they can be planted in a well-prepared site and staked as and when the weather allows – they get a head start in spring, growing away strongly.

Andrew McCoryn and the team at Coleton Fishacre Garden (The National Trust) near Dartmouth, Devon

Here's some clear-cut advice about planting different types of trees.

 Broad-leaved trees should be planted by the end of February because their roots begin to grow much earlier in the year than conifers. Most conifers should be planted by Easter, with two exceptions – the silver fir and the larch. These have a flush of new leaves that can suffer from frost damage. Therefore, plant them a few weeks after Easter. If the ground is frozen, leave well alone. Store your tree in a frost-free place until the ground thaws.

Colin Morgan, Curator of Bedgebury National Pinetum (The Forestry Commission) near Cranbrook, Kent

A real enthusiast, Robert Vernon, travels widely and on one of his European trips; the September flowers of one tree made him stop the car and take a look.

There's one tree I'd like every gardener to know about – *Tilia henryana*. It's a small tree, about the same size as a mountain ash and the leaves are about two and a half times larger than an ordinary lime leaf. Each one is deeply toothed to a depth of 1cm (½in). The spring foliage is silver-pink and there is another flush of growth around Lammas Day (1 August) and that is equally stunning. The really wonderful thing about this tree is the scented ivory-white flowers, which appear in September when very little else is in flower. They're breathtaking. This tree is very hardy, though it dislikes wind.

Robert Vernon of the Bluebell Nursery and Arboretum near Ashby-de-la-Zouch, Leicestershire

Winter gardens have become more popular recently, and the Cambridge Botanic Garden set the trend with theirs several years ago. The coloured stems of *Cornus* – rich greens, warm reds and butter-yellows – are mass planted and they add a real buzz of warmth to this lovely garden tucked into the bustling city of Cambridge.

Once the upper buds begin to open on the shrubs grown for their colourful winter stems, we start pruning. We cut the vigorous plants down to ground level every year (known as stooling). This includes all forms of *Cornus stolonifera* and *Cornus alba*. The less vigorous *Cornus sanguinea* 'Winter Beauty' and 'Midwinter Fire' have a third of their old wood removed. We also cut down the white-bloomed stems of the ghost brambles. Those of *Rubus cockburnianus* are taken down completely, but *R. thibetanus* 'Silver Fern' has only one or two of the old stems removed because it's a slow grower. Our large groups of salixes are cut down alternately, one left, one stooled.

Richard Todd, Head Gardener at Anglesey Abbey Garden (The National Trust), Cambridgeshire

This is a general pruning rule for shrubs of all kinds.

Newly planted shrubs should never be cut back hard, just lightly trim them if they need it. Established spring-flowering shrubs, such as forsythias, should be pruned straight after flowering. However, if the shrub flowers after midsummer, as do buddlejas, fuchsias and perovskias, reduce each strong stem by two thirds in spring and remove any weak growth completely. The following shrubs respond to hard pruning: lilacs, deutzias and philadelphus. If you have an old congested shrub that is badly out of shape. Be brave and prune hard back, but be prepared for failure.

Paul Underwood, Head Gardener at Blickling Hall (The National Trust) near Norwich, Norfolk

Clay soil suits many shrubs and trees once they are established. The golden rule is that new plants should be introduced during spring, not autumn. They will surely die if they have to sit through a cold winter in sticky clay. The head gardener at Batsford does have a solution, however.

When planting a bare-rooted tree on heavy clay soil, don't dig it into a hole, do as the Victorians did and 'mound' plant. Fork the area over, one spit deep and three times as wide as the circumference of the roots. Ameliorate the area with compost or chippings. Lightly firm the soil and, taking a bare-rooted standard, spread the tree's roots over it. Carefully cover with a 50–50 mixture of native and imported soil, firmly making a mound up to the root collar. Stake the lower third of the tree and cover the whole area with a layer of mulch to suppress weeds, keep the soil moist and encourage bio-activity. (A standard tree measures 2m/6ft in height.)

Malcolm MacLachlan, Head Gardener at Batsford Arboretum near Moreton-in-Marsh, Gloucestershire

Many areas in the western half of Britain have acid soil and this extends the range of plants that can be grown. Decorative trees originally from China and Japan thrive in these gardens. The Harold Hillier Gardens and Arboretum, though situated in a mainly alkline area in the south-east of England, enjoys acid soil, which makes the rest of us jealous.

We find that mid- to late February is the best time to mulch our magnolias, camellias and bamboos. We use well-rotted garden compost and spread it out under the tree to the drip line, avoiding the area close to the trunk. This feeds the plant and keeps the area weed free, saving any digging or weeding, which should be avoided underneath camellias and magnolias as they are surface rooted. We grow trilliums under the canopies and they thrive in this rich, humic environment. When the witch-hazels have finished flowering, we tip back the branches to encourage sideshoots; this encourages more flowers next year.

Duncan Goodwin, Head Gardener at The Sir Harold Hillier Gardens and Arboretum (Hampshire County Council), Hampshire

The Higher Garden at Lanhydrock is another area full of acid-loving camellias, rhododendrons, magnolias and azaleas. The rest of the garden contains some fine specimen trees. The head gardener there occasionally has to resort to surgery!

Late on in the year is a good time to thoroughly check your trees for damage. Look for dieback, rotting stems and dead branches. Also check for fungal growth around the trunk and the surrounding areas of ground. All are indicators that all is not well. Check all your tree stakes, loosening the ties if necessary. Consider whether tree surgery is required. Once any remedial work is done, add a low nitrogen, slow-release fertilizer to the area around the tree and then mulch with well-rotted organic material, leaving the trunk clear.

Nigel Teagle, Head Gardener at Lanhydrock (The National Trust) near Bodmin, Cornwall

Keith Marshall loves roses, and Margaret, his wife, has a passion for herbaceous plants. They advocate some serious garden visiting throughout the year.

A garden should be a personal statement. Grow the plants you like, rather than growing what garden designers and other people tell you to grow. Our garden and nursery, though known for old-fashioned roses and herbaceous plants, is interesting during the rest of the year, as every garden should be. Find a large garden near you, preferably one that opens throughout the year, and visit it regularly – about once a month, if possible. This will give you lots of ideas. Rosemoor, The Garden House, Castle Drogo and Marwood are four West Country gardens packed with year-round interest and they're either open over many months or for the whole year.

Keith and Margaret Marshall, owners of Hunts Court Garden and Nursery, North Nibley, Gloucestershire

Don't just go garden visiting for the cream teas though, or in Eastgrove's case, Malcolm's ice-cream. Take a notebook!

Buy two notebooks, one pocket-sized and one large. Use the small book on garden visits, taking a fresh page for each one. Write down the name of the garden and the date of the visit. Search out the plants you like and write their names down. Also write down the plant combinations you like within that garden. Finally, if you buy any plants, record these as well. This will help you to learn the Latin names as well as give you lots of ideas. Use the larger book for your own garden.

Give the different parts of your garden names and designate one page to each. Get into the habit of recording any thoughts and ideas as soon as they come to mind. These notebooks will improve your plant knowledge and your garden.

Carol Skinner of Eastgrove Cottage Garden, Sankyns Green, Worcestershire

Weeds are always a topic of conservation for gardeners, but at Waltham Place they're woven into the planting scheme.

We garden organically and one of the most important aspects of this is to choose the plants that grow naturally in your soil, rather than choosing the plants you want to grow and trying to change the soil for them. Go with what you've got and if you're unsure, visit local gardens to get a feel for the plants that thrive in your area. We also work with our weeds so, for example, rather than trying to eradicate ground elder in badly infested borders, we plant some tough perennials to out-compete it, these include *Geranium* x *psilostemon*, miscanthus, eupatorium, *Stipa calamagrostis* and *Calamagrostis brachytricha*, which are all untroubled by it.

Gert-Jan van der Kolk, Head Gardener at Waltham Place Farm near Maidenhead, Berkshire

Maryline Dyer is French and she uses the walled gardens
at Walmer Castle to create some fun with vegetables and
flowers. There's still time to browse through the seed
catalogues, and vegetables can be as decorative as garden
flowers.

We have three walled gardens at Walmer
Castle and we try to inject an element of fun
by combining flowers and vegetables in
elaborate bedding schemes. We ring the
changes every year, making diagonal lines
one year and straight lines the next, or by
forming squares. We go through the seed
catalogues during the winter and find
colourful and unusual vegetables, such as
purple sweet corn, red cabbages and frilly
lettuces. Then we draw up a plan, reducing
the recommended spacings by half. We get a
lush carpet without any spaces and this
prevents the weeds and cuts down on
watering. We plant everything out in May
and clear the site completely in October. It's
great fun and we enjoy planning it as the rest
of the garden has to be formal.

*Maryline Dyer, Head Gardener at Walmer Castle (English
Heritage), Kent*

Are your plants past their sell-by date? Winter is the perfect time to take stock. A time to remove the old rose that produces five flowers above roof height, to get rid of the woody buddleja at the back of the border and hack out the *Lonicera etrusca* 'Superba' from the side of the house, before it gets any more 'superba' and prevents you getting out of the back door unless you've got a machete.

Don't be afraid to be an aggressive gardener! Be prepared to enjoy your plants while they're at a size to enjoy and while they're performing well. However, when they get too big for your garden or when they cease to look good, have the confidence to remove them. Don't be sentimental, you can always propagate from the old plant and start again. Summer is an ideal time to make the necessary judgements. If you looked critically at your plants then, you can remove them now and look forward to keeping a fresh garden, not one with plants past their peak.

Ian Wright, Head Gardener at Trengwainton (The National Trust) near Penzance, Cornwall

The rose garden at Sudeley Castle contains a wonderful collection of old-fashioned roses that are grown organically. This expert advice comes from Iain Billott who was head gardener there before moving to Cumbria.

- You often make up to 40 cuts when you prune a rose, and blunt secateur blades make for chewed and damaged stems, which let in disease. Sharpen your secateurs every morning. I use a round chainsaw file.

- Before the new leaves emerge, drench all your newly pruned roses and the surrounding soil with a strong solution of winter tar wash. Apply it with a watering can and heavy rose, using two gallons per bush. This kills the black spot spores. Then mulch light soils with a 15cm (6in) layer of cow manure or a mixture of spent mushroom compost and leaf mould to feed the roses and conserve moisture.

Ian Billott, former Head Gardener at Sudeley Castle near Winchcombe, Gloucestershire

Plant bare-root roses in preference to containerized ones. Then you won't infect your garden with the black spot spores from the soil round the rose. Rose nurseries have lots of tightly packed pots placed together and disease is often rife, so your rose (though it may look healthy when you buy it) will almost certainly have suffered from black spot. The next bit of sound advice comes from a great rosarian.

Bare-root roses are easy to establish. When you plant them, prune them hard back - to within 5–7cm (2–3in) from the ground, regardless of type. This prevents wind rock and encourages new growth from the base of the plant, giving you a well-balanced – rather than leggy – rose bush in years to come.

Peter Beales of Peter Beales Roses, Attleborough, Norfolk

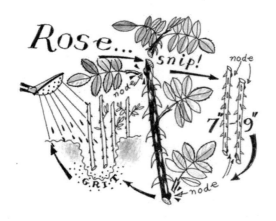

The roses may be bare now, but several clematis provide winter and spring colour.

There are some very good winter- and spring-flowering clematis that grow on sheltered walls. *Clematis cirrhosa* 'Freckles' has creamy pink flowers spotted with maroon. The less floriferous *C. cirrhosa* var. *balearica* has dark ferny leaves and lemon-scented, creamy white flowers. Both flower from mid-winter onwards and are best against warm, sheltered walls. I also recommend *C. armandii*, a leathery-leaved clematis with large, white, single flowers, which appears from early spring onwards. *C. alpina* and *C. chrysocoma* flower slightly later and are useful because they perform on north-facing walls.

David Stuart of Longstock Park Gardens and Nursery, Stockbridge, Hampshire, holder of one of the National Collections of Clematis viticella

Wise gardeners wait for the weather!

When in the last few weeks of winter, don't be too hasty. In cold weather, bide your time and prepare for seed sowing by cleaning pots, labels and greenhouse staging. Cut back any tender plants, including pelargoniums. Make the most of the good days by getting outside and tidying up. Turn over the soil and remove all the debris, adding manure – the frosts will do the rest. Don't work outside in the cold – it's so easy to strain your back. Be patient, wait for warmer weather and then get busy.

Graham Donachie, Head Gardener at Oxburgh Hall (The National Trust) near King's Lynn, Norfolk

Index

Acknowledgements

Gardeners are busy people – and none so busy as Head Gardeners and garden owners. They carry the burden of managing and running a garden on a day-to-day basis. All the contributors have given of their time willingly, sharing their expertise and their enthusiasm with me – however demanding their schedules were. Sometimes we would pass like ships in the night – when they were on the phone I'd be gardening and vice versa. Sometimes it would take several days to make contact at all. Many a time I would have liked a Tardis – to time travel to your gardens and see the things you described. Some of the best gems were given to me by modest individuals who thought their contribution unimportant. It wasn't! Thank you everyone for your hands on advice – I've enjoyed every minute of talking to you and I've learnt such a lot from you all...

Val Bourne is a writer, broadcaster and plantswoman who has been editing the Seeds of Wisdom column for the *Daily Telegraph* gardening supplement since it was launched in 2000. She has a totally organic garden in Hook Norton, Oxfordshire where she specialises in hardy perennials and cottage garden flowers.

Allan Drummond regularly contributes illustrations to the *Daily Telegraph* gardening supplement as well as writing and illustrating his own books for children.